Running by the Mile
10 Steps for a Successful Trucking Business

By Bruce Outridge

Dedicated to Those in Transportation

Running By The Mile is published by Bruce Outridge Productions a division of Outridge Enterprises Inc. All articles, pictures, illustrations, and content are copyright of Outridge Enterprises Inc. and may not be reproduced in whole or in part in any means without the written consent of the publisher or their assigned agents.

©2012 Outridge Enterprises Inc.
Published by Bruce Outridge Productions / Outridge Enterprises Inc.
Layout and design, illustrations, and photographs by Bruce Outridge Productions
Content, articles, and information provided by Outridge Consulting Services / Division of Outridge Enterprises Inc.

Publishers Mailing Address:

Outridge Enterprises Inc.
700-20 North Shore Blvd. West
Burlington, Ontario, L7T 1A1

Online purchases available through our websites at www.outridge.ca | www.bruceoutridge.com | www.outridgeenterprises.ca

To purchase copies by phone please call 289-337-2630. Also available at approved retailers.

ISBN NUMBER: 978-0-9869205-6-1

1st printing United States

10 Success Steps for Owner Operators

How Many Times have you Been Told "No!"

How many times have you been told no? I'm not talking about keeping your hands out of the cookie jar type of no, I'm talking about people telling you can't do certain things, or you're not good enough, or you don't have the talent, or experience. We hear these things everyday, people challenging us from moving forward. Many times looking for a job or position we hear this from recruiters, and we start believing it ourselves. How many times did someone tell you that you didn't have enough experience for the type of work you wanted and after that you stopped looking at the industry. How many talented people have moved on to other areas because someone didn't give them a chance to prove themselves? I have been told these things many times through out my life.

I was told at a very young age that I wasn't good enough to make it though school. After all I had trouble getting past grade 4. I was bored and told the same thing through out high school before dropping out. I finally got my diploma. My doctor as a kid told me if I didn't stop eating I wouldn't make it past the age of 35. I am now 49 years old and very healthy. I was told I wasn't good enough to become an artist in high school. I own an illustration business to this day. When I decided to get into trucking I was told don't get into that industry, there's no money there. In the industry I was told don't do this or don't do that, you'll never make it. I have been in the transportation industry for 30 years and have had a very successful career. Folks, it is all crap! After a while with everyone telling you "no" you start to believe it yourself, and there lies the first problem. I used to believe what everyone was telling me also and it took me a long time to get over it. Once you believe in yourself and start telling yourself you CAN do things is when they start happening. Almost everything I have been told no to, I have completed successfully.

So how do you start telling yourself yes? Take a look at your track record and make some notes as to the accomplishments you have achieved. Look at where you want to go and see where you need some help in experience or expertise. Sometimes seeing all of these things in one place helps boost our spirits and gets us moving on the right track. If you are trying to get a job then let the potential employer know the type of person you are and your work ethic. That may replace some experience and encourage someone to take a chance on you. Maybe there is a way of gaining some experience through another program. If you're a recruiter, think differently about that next candidate. Of course stay within your hiring criteria, but also look at the person. Many times business is done on a hunch or gut feeling. If you have a gut feeling that a person is good, but the experience is lacking find a way to get that person in the door. The help now will bring in strong loyalty and work ethic down the road. People just need to hear a yes once in a while. We've all made mistakes in the past, it doesn't mean we can't have a bright future. I know I did!

Being told "NO" has never been truer than in the business area of trucking and Owner Operators. Ask anyone at any truck stop if you can make money as an Owner Operator and you will be told "NO"! Even the people recruiting you don't believe it. I have seen recruiters that their job is to hire Owner Operators who stand out in presentations and say I wouldn't do it. There jobs are numbers of candidates not your business success.

If there is no possible way of you making it as an Owner Operator then why are there thousands of Owner Operators operating across North America to this day. Go to any truck show across the country and see hundreds of Owner Operators showing off their pride and joy. So who do you listen to, who do you talk to get the facts? You listen to people who have been in business before, you listen to people who have been in the seat and understand the industry of transportation, and you listen to your own common sense. It's absolutely true that 50% of all Owner Operators fail. Folks that statistic is alive in any business whether it be an Internet business, a dress maker's shop, or a toy store. The statistics go up for those businesses under five years old. Does that mean you shouldn't try, does that mean anytime a business starts to have tough times they should shut down? The answer of course is no. Entrepreneurs, small business owners, and Owner Operators are the type of people that when something isn't working you don't give up, you adjust your plan, you keep tweaking your operation, you find answers to questions you have. When you ask those questions to other drivers at the truck stop, they won't tell you they failed, they'll blame everything under the sun but them, the company, the fuel prices, dispatch, everyone but them.

This book is written not just to give you business information to help you succeed, but to give you a vision, to show you that anyone can make it if they stay disciplined, keep tweaking their operation to make it better, and learn how to keep the engine of their business running smoothly. This book is also a leadership book because in my mind anyone can learn the practical elements of running a business. You can be taught how to have good time management, you can hire a bookkeeper to keep your business in good order, those things can be taught. However it is very hard to teach someone intuition, to be entrepreneurial, to want to be in business, to keep their vision in front of them even when things seem to be going wrong. This my friends is business mentality and that is what makes someone successful. Now remember success is not about the money, you want to make money, but success is about having a successful business, running profitably, and creating a business that can be built for the future. There will always be truck drivers whether on the road or in space ships because transportation is a core industry, it's everywhere. Our economy would shut down if not for transportation, we touch everything that consumers have. There will always be Owner Operators because their will always be people that want control of their future. Smart Owner Operators always make money because they have a handle on their business.

If you follow the steps in this book you will have the foundation to get started as a successful business owner, but much like a professional driver, your job is not finished because you read this book, you have to keep honing your business to run the best it can. That will take years of analysis, and self motivation but it can be done. If your goal is to own one truck or twenty down the road this book is for you. I wish you luck and continued success with your new business venture.

Running by the Mile - 10 Steps to a Successful Trucking Business

Step 1

Is This the Industry for You?

S hould you become and Owner Operator or stay as a professional driver? I wish I could tell you to just do this or go here, but in reality I can't. Life doesn't work that way and either does the trucking industry. I am sure your personal life doesn't work that way either. The problem is that this is a choice you need to make based on goals and dreams you have for yourself and your family. What may be the right choice for me may not be the right choice for you? For instance early in my career when I was still pumping gas, that's when gas stations pumped gas, I was told by an older person not to get into the trucking industry, that you couldn't make any money at it. Thirty years later not only have I had a successful career in the industry, but have met many friends along the way, seen some great parts of our country, and supported my family. If I had listened to that person I may still be pumping gas to this day. So you certainly have to have your own mindset as to where you want to go in the future. That being said, is it better to become an Owner Operator or stay as a professional driver, really the choice is up to you.

I have been both in my lifetime and for different reasons than many of you may have. I was an Owner Operator in the furniture industry before moving to the freight side of the industry. My career path took me to work with some great companies that paid well and were somewhat specialized in the products they hauled. This caused me not to have that drive to be an Owner Operator but to move up the ranks in the corporate world. If I had worked at regular transport companies I may have had more incentive to become an Owner Operator again. So the choice is most certainly a personal one based on your goals. Much of the choice will be do you want to drive for your whole career or do you have notions of moving into the office of a company in safety or some other important department? Once you have your goals set in that area you can start looking at the type of companies and positions that will get you to that point. You may be able to access some of them now or you may have to get experience first and try for those positions later. As I have mentioned work with your career path first and the lifestyle you want. The rest will fall into place, most of all don't listen to just anyone. Many think they know, but they don't. The person that told me not to get into the business obviously didn't work at the same places that I did, or he may still be in it.

Recently I received a call from a gentleman that owned his own truck and was looking to change carriers due to too much waiting time. He had read a magazine column I wrote and because I was local to him decided to give me a call to see if I knew any good carriers to work with. As we discussed opportunities available to him a couple times I mentioned a carrier and his reaction was,"We had a guy who came from there and he said they weren't very good." When I asked him what was bad about them he didn't know, just that what he was told. As our conversation came to a close I urged him to give those other carriers a call as I believe they would have been a good fit for him and his unit.

As I hung up the phone I thought to myself there goes another one. As a consultant and previous driver and Owner Operator I have been through the same issues as most drivers. We listen to those on the road and make decisions based on hearsay instead of rock solid information.

When I was beginning my own career I was told the same thing don't become a truck driver and here I am 30 years later with a good name and successful career in the industry. If I had listened to that guy earlier in my life I might still be pumping gas since that was what I was doing before the shift. Of course I would be unemployed now because everything is self-serve. As a consultant I hear this all the time, drivers saying, "I heard by another driver at the truck stop you can't make any money as an Owner Operator." If you can't make money why are so many people doing it? To illustrate this further I have talked with some Owner Operators at the same company and one will say they are going bankrupt and another will say they are making money. Is it the company?

I tell people all the time, STOP LISTENING TO THOSE WHO DO NOT KNOW! I am not saying don't listen to other people's opinions, what I am saying is talk to people who know what they are talking about. If it is a carrier go talk to the person at the company, get the pay package, ask those questions about down time and other important issues. If you listen to the guy at the truck stop he won't tell you that the reason he has been sitting is because he isn't reliable. The guy at the truck stop won't tell you that he doesn't do a good job of running his business and has no idea where his money goes. As reporters say, "Get the facts and nothing but the facts." Once you have the facts and have had discussions with company officials you can now weigh the information you received at the truck stop to see if it is true or not. Then you can make a sound decision. As they say get it directly from the horses mouth! Success begins with using your head and feeling in your gut to decide what's right for you, not the guy at the truck stop.

Now that I have you not listening to people I want you to listen to me, trucking isn't for everyone. If you are a driver moving into Owner Operator then I'm not telling you anything new, however if you are new to this industry then you need to decide if this is the lifestyle for you. In trucking there isn't a whole lot of down time because no one is paid if the wheels aren't turning. Add being sent places you have never seen before, and not having a steady schedule to know when you will be home can be challenging at best. For someone new coming into the industry as an Owner Operator it can be a challenge to find a balance between your life and your business. This is especially true if there are children involved or a family at home. I myself have missed many birthday parties and major events due to life on the road, but in the end I don't regret them because I have had a very successful career and they were worth the sacrifice. With all the obstacles involved in trucking how do you make it work for you so you don't feel that it is choking you rather than helping you succeed. We all know people who have come into this industry thinking they were going to be successful but couldn't get over the factor of being away from home. The secret is inside you, you have to decide on the type of lifestyle you want to have and what is important for you to be present at. The trick is in the balance of priorities. Many Owner Operators will just take time off for anything that is family related. That may work for them but won't help their pocket book. To be honest with you there is some family functions I would rather avoid and trucking has been a great excuse for those ones when needed. On the other side are the Owner Operators who are so involved with succeeding with their business they go at it 150% all the time and never slow down or take a break.

This is especially true for the single guys that have no family at home and focus on making the big money. You have to have balance. Figure out what you like to do and what is important for you to attend. If it something like a graduation or other important event book it off, those times don't come by too often. Other events you may miss or try to schedule at times when you know you'll be home if you can predict your schedule. With Skype and other technological products you probably won't miss as much as you think. For your own sanity find things you like to do on the road, and try to find ways you can to participate while away. When I used to get a day off I would find a park and go canoeing or sightseeing within reason. I have seen people with bicycles on the back of their truck and so forth. I used to go to the gym on the road so I bought a membership that could be used across North America. I would call and see if truck parking was near by and went to some great gyms from New York to Houston. Take your hobbies with you and you will find a different perspective to your work life balance. Get creative with your work habits and try to include your hobbies as much as possible. Don't just sit in your truck for a day watching trucks pull into the truck stop because you're laid over, enjoy your surroundings and you may find that trucking gives you a whole new outlook on life.

Recently while eating in a truck stop I began talking with a man and his Grandfather that were heading up to Sudbury to go fishing. Both talked about the cabin in the woods where the fish are fresh, and is accessible by boat or pontoon plane only. While talking about their trip I began to admire the long standing relationship that was very prominent between them. It made me think back to my life on the road and the family time that I sacrificed to be a professional truck driver.

As professional drivers and Owner Operators attending family commitments, scheduling time with family, and other personal interests can get lost in the shuffle of trying to make a buck. Add to that the lifestyle of a professional driver being on the road all the time and it is almost impossible to find time to spend with loved ones. When I was driving steady I was coaching my son's hockey team, had a girl in skating, plus all the school issues going on. The only holiday that I put any effort to attending was Christmas. So how do you balance family time and work duties while on the road?

In my work now as a business owner, consultant, and entrepreneur I find it just as difficult to take time off as I did while on the road. You never know where your next dollar is coming from or how far away it is from being in your bank account. Much like being an Owner Operator. As an Owner Operator you are trying to keep up with payments, maintenance, and other duties trying to keep that truck running down the road. Scheduling family time becomes secondary, but in reality it should come first. Where I see many people go wrong is that they think to have good family time you need to be available at every moment of the day. If Johnny has soccer at 4pm you need to be there. As much as we all want to see our children grow it is just as important to let them know that you are working hard for them. The important games are the ones you need to be at, not the practices.

One thing that I learned is that you have to schedule that time off. Plan it out with your family at the beginning of the year so that all the important holidays are covered and if you're available after that then those will slot in where able. Then run your schedule for the rest of the year. This will help your family know when you will be available, but also help your income by knowing when you will be scheduled off helping you with maintenance schedules and more. Time management and organization are the key to running a successful business no matter what the product or service is and scheduling that time off is just as important.

Connecting With Family on the Road

One of the largest challenges for professional drivers and owner operators is time away from family and friends. Life on the road can be lonely, hectic, and frustrating all at the same time. Many times you have no control over the location of your loads, when you return home, or the time away from family. The challenge increases based on the make up of your family, for instance if you are single you may not care about time away from home, if you are married you may try to get home more often but can still manage life on the road. However when you have children the younger they are the harder it is to be on the road and gone from the family. The challenge for most drivers is that the time at which they are hitting their stride in their career is usually the same time that they start to have children and want to spend time with them. This can be a challenge like no other. There are a couple of ways to handle the problem without upsetting the whole apple cart.

I went through this when I was driving so I understand the challenges of the road and a family. When my kids came into the picture I was at the height of my career in trucking. I had my own truck and trailer was running where I wanted to run and making good money, life was good. At first it was fine to be on the road but then the tug on the heart strings came along and I was looking at other options to be home more. I switched companies after a while, but wasn't home a whole lot more. Once trucking is in your blood it is hard to get it out. That being said it is important to work with what you've got. If you enjoy the road then stay there and figure out how to adapt because you won' be happy if you stay home.

One of the things that work the best is consistency. I used to call my family every night when I was on the road around the same time. They got used to that phone call and would have all their news from the day ready to go when I called. Make them part of your life. I'm not talking about just pictures in your truck but them get them involved with your truck. If you wash it yourself have them help so they develop a pride in it, take them to the truck shows and help them understand the life of a professional driver. Have them track you on the road. Create a map on a board and have them put pins in where you have been each day, kind of like tracking Santa. With social media and Skype you can now see them face to face that can be a great boost to those on the road for extended periods. The last thing is to do your best to be at the important functions. Be part of their lives whenever possible. Make the extra effort to get home for weekend games and other important functions. When you are home, be there for your family, you'll be glad you did!

Running by the Mile - 10 Steps to a Successful Trucking Business

Step 2

Goal Setting Your Career

In extreme sports you are putting much of your faith in your equipment, guide experience, and other factors such as training and conditioning. In business you are putting your faith in your products and services, marketing, commitment level, and work ethic. There is always the possibility for something to go wrong. For those of us in business things probably will go wrong at some point, but that shouldn't stop you from going into business. Just like the folks that do extreme sports preparation and training are steps that make the sport safer for the person participating. Ask yourself who feels safer, a person making their first sky jump from an airplane, or the person that has jumped four hundred times?

Starting off in business is scary for everyone and for those that can stick it out past the first couple of years usually can find their track and begin to find success. The scary part is commitment and jumping off the cliff. The secret to the success of your business is planning. Just as a sky jumper plans where to jump, where they may land, what gear they need and so on, a business owner needs to plan how they will reach their intended goal, what products and services they will offer, and how they will market themselves to the world. We all take stabs and try things, but overall the successful businesses have a plan written down that is showing them the way to their goals. There may be construction on that road now and then but you will eventually arrive at your intended destination. If you don't plan for success you may find yourself in areas you don't want to be.

So if you are thinking of a going into business and wonder if you are going to make it or not, the answer is yes, you may or may not make it? By creating a plan you have given yourself the best possible chance for success.

If you ask most owner operators what the goals for their business are most would tell you to make it down the road safely and come out with some money in their pockets. While that may make a lofty operational goal it doesn't help you in the long run to be successful. Some mention just making their truck payments, others want family time and so on. These are all fine goals, but are they structured enough to get you to where you want to be? The answer is no, goals to most people mean dreaming and that is why they don't usually work. Goals need specific items in order to work and to do it right require planning and soul searching in a quiet place when you are rested and alert. So what kind of goals should be important to you as an owner operator?

I am assuming you got into business to be successful, I am also assuming you plan on being in business for many years to come. That being said I am strongly in favour of having short, medium, and long term goals. I also like to set monetary and personal time goals. Let's talk about the time goals first, take out a piece of paper on a day when you are rested and relaxed, if married this is a good exercise to do with your spouse as well and figure out where you want your business to be in 6 months, 1 year, and 5 years. A goal for that area may be to pay off your truck, trade up to a newer truck, may be even have additional trucks. May be your goal in 5 years will be to retire or slow down a bit, if so how do you do that, what needs to be in place for that to happen, how will you get there? A six month goal may be to increase revenue by 5% over the last quarter and so forth. Maybe your goal is to increase your personal time at home, how will you accomplish that, can you get a second driver; manage a small fleet of trucks you own as opposed to driving one full time. What will get you to that mark?

Monetary goals are the same but are even better because they do two things; they force you to look at your numbers, and they work in conjunction with time goals which helps you succeed. To set monetary goals look at your most important paper that you have, your profit and loss statement. Start there and figure out where you want to be in a certain time frame such as the ones above. Do you want to cut certain areas of expenses, maybe you need to make more miles, etc?

To make the goal setting experience work you need to put hard numbers on everything. So if your goal is to increase your profit margin by 10 % also include a figure such as $1000. Then you have a hard goal to work with. The second thing you must do is put a date on your goals. This helps give you a specific time in which to work on your goal. With these specifics you can now create an action plan to achieve the goals making you successful. Just going through this process will put you in the 10% category of successful business owners. You know what they say, if you fail to plan, then you plan to fail!

All right, you have made the decision to become your own boss, to own your own truck, to build your career as a business owner, but how do you go about it? As with any business the fun part of the business is setting the business, dreaming about what can be, envisioning the future in your own unique way. The reality is that once you have completed the setup stage many business owners realize that the actual activity of being in business can be daunting and downright scary. So how do you prepare yourself for the business you have dreamed about, how do you help ensure you will be successful after the setup stage. The answer to that is planning!

You must plan how you will get from point A to point B, it won't just happen without work and certainly won't work without a plan. Before you even get started in business you should have worked out a business plan to help you with your business success. The business plan will tell you how you should set up your business, who will be involved in the operation either daily or on a sporadic basis. The plan will help you decide how you will do business, who you will run for, how many miles you will need and how much you need to earn to break even and be profitable. If you don't know those numbers then you are just floating through business without a clear idea of where you should be going. Without the proper numbers that are shown in a profit and loss statement you will not have the information required for you to make important decisions such as should I start trading my truck due to high maintenance costs, low fuel mileage and so on. These are important decisions that need to be made based on fact and proper accounting rather than by just having a feeling that it may be time to buy that new truck. Do your homework and prepare for your business and you will have a successful business. Float by the seat of your pants and the point you land may not be what you had envisioned.

The important thing especially when starting out however is to follow your game plan. Many people especially entrepreneurs, marketing specialists, owner operators, etc. have great intentions of creating a marketing plan and implementing it, however when they don't see any results they start to slip into that complacency stage assuming nothing is working. This is very true especially with social media where you hear that all you have to do is sign on and then people will flood to your business. Nothing is further from the truth.

Anyone starting any kind of long term project, business, or marketing effort will need to realize that it may take anywhere from 6 months to a year or more to start seeing the fruits of their labour. The important part is to keep working at it with all of your might. This has happened to me many times through our various business ventures.

I remember when I started my blog and every week posted an article wondering if anyone was even reading them. Then out of the blue I would get a reply from someone with a comment. The same thing happened on Twitter when I first signed on, zero followers and I didn't follow anyone, heck I barely ever signed on. But I put it on my to-do list anyway and kept posting. Today I have 15 people following my comments on Twitter. Sure it's not huge like Lady Gaga, and I'm sure if I spent even more time telling people what I ate for lunch and giving more comments on subjects I could gain a lot more. My newsletter has just started bringing in clients who have been following me for a year. People are ready to listen at different times in their lives and if you keep moving forward you will be there when they need you.

The point is to keep working, and even more important is that I am following my original game plan for social media marketing. I've used social media as an example but I have found the same ground can be gained through other areas by just staying with the plan. Your gut will tell you when you're ready to grow, so stick to the plan. I enjoy reading my horoscope once in a while, I'll read it and it will say "things are going on in the background that you don't know about". Then down the road I will talk with someone and they will ask "if my ears were burning" because they were recommending me to someone for an opportunity.

So if you're the type of person to let your guard down when you don't see things happening then I suggest you take those scrap pieces of paper that you wrote those original goals on ,dust them off and get back to work on them. The success in hitting goals is making sure you follow through with the work part. What if with your hard work you are able to make it, you are successful, you're no longer a statistic of the business world. But what if tomorrow never comes?

That title is the making of a great song by Garth Brooks in the country genre, but it also the end of a career and life to an unassuming young man. For those of you in Southern Ontario have probably heard of a young man involved in an accident in a rural part of Simcoe Ontario. The accident resulted in eleven people dying including the truck driver. This horrific crash happened early morning on a country highway. The young truck driver had just called his wife to say he would be home in an hour or so.

I bring up this terrible tragedy to show you the importance of the moment. The importance of doing today what you need to do to be successful in business, career, or personal life. I hear so many people say that they will do that tomorrow, or will work on it down the road, but what if tomorrow never comes? This happens to all of us but at some time you need to make sure you have control of your life. Life goes on and only the strong survive. So what does all of this have to do with trucking?

In the transportation industry the rumblings are beginning to start again, fuel prices are rising, freight is there but at what quality, and drivers seem to be in a bubble as to what will happen in the industry next. So as an Owner Operator you have two choices, you can join the crowd and start bellyaching over all the things happening in our industry or you can take a stand and decide to be successful. I personally would do the second one but again, the choice is yours. What will you do?

Plan! If you have been riding along at the edge of your seat and hoping for the best now is the time to stop. Take a good hard look at your business, is it where you want to be, take a look at your family life, is that where you would like it to be? Do you connect with family while on the road, do you have the right business practices happening in your business so that you can succeed? Is there a proper management team in place to make sure you are making quality decisions and moving your business and career in a forward direction. If the answer to these and hundred other questions you may ask is "no" then you have work to do. You can't control life, you can't foresee the future, but you can make sure you have done everything in your power to have a successful life. I ask you the question again, what if tomorrow never comes?

What about the guys who are afraid of moving on, or are in a rut and are afraid to make that leap like the guy on edge of the cliff? Do you ever get in a rut and the days just seem to go by? Some people don't even realize they are in the rut, they just go about their business not thinking about tomorrow. What about the guys who get to the end of that work life and find they have nothing left to work for. At that end of life things change in a different direction, you start holding on, afraid to let go not wanting to give up that position that you have created for a lifetime. This happens to many of us, we trudge through life not sure where we're going. If you're lucky you notice it in time to make changes, if not then you hope for the best.

This happened to me in my driving career I had reached a high level of satisfaction with the company. I had a number of years of seniority, good vacation time and benefits. I never drove trucks older than two years old and was dedicated to my own trailer. I was on dedicated runs that gave me secure miles and income. Everything a professional driver could want, except for one thing. I had stopped growing. Up to that point I had been working hard to make a name for myself as the best professional driver I could be. I kept the truck polished, delivered on time, and was not afraid to step up and take that extra load to help the team. Once I hit that mark of having all the attributes I was trying to gain the boredom process began to set in. At that point you have two choices, you can continue to follow your current program and keep a stable lifestyle and income or you can turn the whole thing upside down and try to find a way to make yourself grow again.

Now when I suggest you turn your life upside down that is meant tongue and cheek. I don't expect you to quit your job, put your family in the street and hang out at coffee shops. I do want you to look at what fueled that fire when you started in your career and try to capture that spirit again. Many times this can be done by creating a bucket list of things you hoped to achieve through your career and personal life. Maybe the best place to start is in your own operation, what can be improved, what can be changed, what can be discarded? Have you been on that dedicated run too long and need to move into other areas? Are you thinking about getting into the safety department or some other administrative department?

Maybe now is the time to start asking some questions and improving where needed. The only person that can fuel that passion is you. Like any fire that fuel for the fire starts at the bottom of the fire and that's where it has to start with you. Sometimes making a change requires drastic measures, just like starting a fire sometimes requires lighter fluid!

I was listening to a song on the radio the other day by singer / songwriter Brad Paisley. In the song he talks about what he would say to himself if he was looking back to the days when he was 17 years old and writing a letter to look out for the dips in life that cause so much pain. One line in the song talks about the goal of any 17 year old to be Friday night and whatever party was going on at the time. I am sure that was the same for many of us and it certainly was for me. I found it funny how things change in our lives such as goal setting, viewing the future, and so on. Have we changed from those days really?

In my day in high school certainly the goal was to get to Friday night and the party. Looking a week out was not even in the cards. As I got a little older my goals stretched to two to four years down the road. I think that is normal for most folks and many of us that teach goal setting teach 6 months to 5 years depending on the situation, but is that far enough? Where I see many entrepreneurs lacking is that their goals don't go far enough. They may go out five years but those are working goals. To really hit your vision and keep yourself motivated for the long term you need to go out 10, 15, or more years. What will your life be like then? What types of milestones will you have hit at that point?

Many entrepreneurs because they are focusing on 5 year goals stop if they feel that will be too hard to keep going, when really you have just started. Think about it this way, you're 40 years old starting your business. You have the recommended 6 month, 1 year, and 5 year goals set. You think that is long term. If you are going to retire at 65 that is 25 years from the time you started your business. So five years is not even a quarter of the way. If you take 5 years to get your business started you will think you're a failure, give up, and miss on the 15 years of success you could have had. So think of goals setting as far as you can. The 5 year goals are operational goals, they are not achievement goals. Those visions of success at the end will be the same visions keeping you motivated in the beginning.

I hope the information in this chapter helps you make the decision to either get into the industry and move on as a business owner or find what is important to you and live your life to the fullest. The only person that can do that for you is you and creating that fire within you is ignitable with the right amount of passion and enthusiasm. Maybe you just need a little lighter fluid?

Running by the Mile - 10 Steps to a Successful Trucking Business

Step 3

Truck Training Requirements

Many people coming into our industry think that by having the proper license to drive a truck they have all the training they need to do the job properly. The truth is and most experienced drivers will tell you the same thing that you have not even begun to become the professional driver you need to be. It's like deciding on a school based on price. You shop around, pick one that fits your budget to find out you only get two hours of in-truck training per week when you need 40. They haven't lied they may offer truck training but fall down under the other standards. So thinking because you have your license that you are qualified when really you are missing half the equation. A qualified individual is someone who is trained, has experience, and knowledge. As a newly licensed driver you may have been trained, you may have partial knowledge, but you are missing the experience part of the equation. This part will take time to achieve and much patience. Getting in with a company that understands the new truck driver and the types of situations you will come across, can be a great benefit to the new industry professional. This is why the larger carriers are probably best for the new person who needs a little guidance once their training is completed. The rule of thumb in the industry is that the person with 5-10 years of experience has sufficient knowledge and experience to be qualified. The guiding factor for recruiters is 2 years experience. That is the bar set by most companies as the time required to understand the finer points of trucking. Of course this time line does move depending on the product or services the company offers, and operational situation, do they have trainers on staff, do they have an in-house training program and so on.

So if you are new to the industry know that you will not be considered a professional driver for at least 5 years, but you will be qualified after 2 years. Of course at this point we are just talking about truck driving in general. If you are an Owner Operator you can expect to add on to that by at least 2 years. So lets say that you are brand new out of school ready to be a truck driver in the industry. Up to now you have 8 weeks of training and have acquired your license. You want to become an Owner Operator and manage to sign on with a company that takes new candidates right away. You will need some time to get used to truck driving, you will need time to learn the rules of business, and you will need time to understand the industry as a whole. Trying to learn that all at the same time will probably sink you with all that is required to know. So what do you do? Find a professional to help set up your business properly for you. Keep good notes and learn about the industry and situations that you will come across, and finally work on your own skills of time management, safe driving, and more to make sure you are operating to the best of your abilities. The last part is to have patience, this will take time, and you will make mistakes. The important part is to learn from them.

As I speak with many new drivers thinking about going to training schools many times I find they don't look far enough ahead in their careers to make choices that will affect them later. For instance they get approved for retraining and then settle on getting a lower license instead of going for the one that will give them the most bang for their buck. Settling in the training portion will greatly affect your opportunities for employment down the road. Many of the folks I talk with in training sessions realize the downfalls of settling on attaining a "D" based license when an "A" License would offer so much more in job opportunities

Now don't get me wrong there is nothing wrong with a "D" license, but I always suggest to people that it is a stepping stone. By staying at the level of "D" license you will confine yourself to job opportunities in the local market, driving straight trucks, construction vehicles and more. With a "D" license you will for the most part do more lifting than those with a higher license just because of vehicle configuration. Straight trucks operate primarily around city centres and multiple and small deliveries are a normal daily routine. You will find down the road as you get older that the "D" license limits your employment opportunities because employers need younger workers to fill those roles so they can keep up with the demand of the job. Unfortunately when this become apparent to most the damage is done and it gets to be too late to start retraining for another career.

An "A" license however gives you the best of both worlds and gives you much more opportunity for employment changes down the road. With an "A" license you can still drive lower class licensed vehicles but you always keep your options open. Vehicles using a class "A" license carry heavier freight therefore most of it is hands off forklift freight, which means you can work for the company without worrying about trying to lift and deliver freight when you get into your older years. You have the same opportunities of working local or long distance but there are many more carriers looking for class "A" licensed drivers than there are looking for "D" licensed drivers. With many companies the opportunities for employment are with long haul work and class 8 vehicles. Some companies don't even have straight trucks.

So if you are looking at training for driving a truck then it is in your best interest to find a place that offers you the best training available and to get a license that will take you as far as possible in the industry. Getting a "D" license because you think you will only work construction with a dump truck to find that you can't get hired because they want you to pull a float trailer behind it and you need an "A" license will make a big difference in pay scale and opportunity. Don't limit yourself for the sake of saving a buck.

For those of you keeping up with the latest industry news you may have heard the Ministry of Transportation is allowing road tests to be taken in a truck with an automatic transmission. While this move has its own positive and negative components I believe the new rule is trying to help allow more people to enter the industry and battle the driver shortage. Whether that is good or bad is yet to be seen.

What I'm concerned with and most should be is when an applicant applies for a position with a company will they be able to safely handle the equipment owned by the employer or will it cause people to start lying on resumes to get the job? This is something that used to go on in the past on various fronts. Like the guy who said he hauled steel regularly and rolled the truck on his first load, or the guy who said he could drive through all sorts of weather and hid in Pennsylvania for a whole week because it was raining. There are all sorts of stories like this across the nation of people trying to get a job without the experience and knowledge to perform it safely. So what is the point here?

The point is that passing the exam at the Ministry is one thing but safely performing the position you are applying for is another. There is a vicious circle of trying to get experience when no one will hire you because you don't have the experience. I have been in that circle of frustration myself. There is a light at the end of the tunnel however and that is by being truthful to the company you will be working for. Not every company has large training programs, but any decent company will answer your questions, so be honest with your information, don't be afraid to ask. Although I have been talking about driving here this goes for load securement, equipment operation, and trip planning. My saying to myself was, "It is always better to look stupid in the yard than in front of the customer." If you aren't sure of how to do something ask, don't pretend you know and then have a problem down the road. Most companies worth their salt will be willing to help someone who is willing to learn, asks questions to be safe, and is trying their best to be a true professional in our industry. Just because you don't have the skill set now doesn't mean you can't learn it, just be willing to learn. Ask yourself which one looks worse, the driver who asks his company how to properly load the trailer, or the driver who pretends to know and rolls it down the road because it wasn't loaded properly? The true professional driver knows the answer. Be a true professional by being willing to learn and you can break out of the cycle of not having the experience faster than you think.

Life is divided up into different classes, it always has been that way and the world seems to work that way. We can go back to the beginning of time and see the formation through slavery and more. I am not saying I agree with it, but that is the way it is and hopefully we will continue working towards meeting people where they are in life and allow them to be who they are. You are probably asking why I bring this up and what does it have to do with trucking?

In the earlier days of the trucking business everyone was regarded as a cowboy, no matter how hard working you were, how good natured, everyone was labeled the same, a cowboy, one class, low! Movies from the seventies which I truly enjoy watching where everyone is dressed like some crazy gear jammer didn't help the driver image very much. If you believe the movies we gambled and drank beer at all the truck stops, and pinched waitress's behinds as they walked by our tables. All waitresses looked like people that would go out to your truck in a moments notice. I am not saying that didn't happen I am just saying it didn't happen everywhere to everyone. Overtime we have come to realize that not all truckers are cowboys, many are just hard working individuals trying to feed their families and make a decent living. Most waitresses are just good people that work very hard and are feeding their families. So what forms our image to the public? If we just go about our jobs each day what will create a positive image to the public, management, or other coworkers? It all comes down to how you deal with people. It comes down to how you do your job every day. It takes time to be known as the person you are.

What can you do to improve your image if it hasn't been as shiny as it should have been? Raise the bar, starting today aim for a higher goal. Lets assume you are a "B" level driver at your company. You get some respect but you have been late a few times and even though you have explained the reasons for your tardiness people don't have total trust in you. You can blame others for the way they see you, or you can look at your track record and see if the problem lies with you. If the lateness comes from poor time management then you need to work on that.

If you stop being late, if you are eager to work as a team player you will find your image improving, therefore making you into an "A" level driver over time. Remember you are not being judged by what you did this week, you are being judged by what you have done over time. Our whole industry has been judged by what people have done in the past both good and bad. Here is a perfect example of how our industry touches others.

It's Tuesday morning and I am swimming from end to end of the massive pool for my morning swim. Normally I have the pool to myself due to the time of day, but this morning I am joined by another person who has taken up the other side of the pool. We both swim our laps and every once in a while take a break at the deep end of the pool. On this particular break the women decides to strike up a conversation and we carry on about the weather as most people do. She asks what I do for a living and I tell her about my various businesses and what they entail. After mentioning that I have been in the transportation industry for over thirty years and drove a transport truck for twenty five of those thirty years her eyes light up. After some more brief conversation she tells me about her early childhood. Apparently when she was a child her family grew up in poverty. They were living in the United States at the time and were a very hard working but poor family. Although I don't know the details the women shared with me that she was selected as a recipient of a scholarship to go to school. The sponsor of the scholarship was the American Trucking Association also known as the "ATA". She is now in her retirement years and is well off with cottages in the Muskokas, and a vacation place in Florida. She feels she owes much of the success in her life to the truckers of this world for giving her that chance to be more than she felt she could have been if it wasn't for the scholarship. She has a great respect for the men and women of the highway and makes sure to always flash her lights and leave room to let a big rig into the lane in front of her. When she told me that I yelled, "FINALLY, WE GOT ONE!" We have gotten through to one of the many four wheelers in our life time.

You're probably wondering why I shared that story with you, what does swimming have to do with transportation? The reason I shared that story is to let you know that because you are driving a truck doesn't mean that you are not helping humanity on a whole. Although this was the American Trucking Association it could well have been the Ontario Trucking Association, or Manitoba Trucking Association, or any of the other major associations here in Canada. You as a driver may not always see the big picture of how people are helped on a daily basis, but know that you are helping people. Look at it this way you are helping people daily in bringing them products that they can use in their daily lives. Your company may give money and donations to charities and also be part of a larger organization such as the Ontario Trucking Association. The Ontario Trucking Association may be part of a larger group again such as the Canadian Trucking Alliance. That larger organization may give away a certain amount of money in the way of scholarships, aid, or other types of donations.

So as you can see you are just one small piece of a much larger puzzle. You are helping people everyday just by doing your job. When you company has "Jean Fridays" or "United Way Mondays" then you are helping people. Look at my friends in Caledonia; they hold a food drive each year bringing tons of food to their local food banks and people in need. The point is that you should feel good about what you are doing for the world while you are doing your job. Whether you realize it or not you are helping your local charities, your country, and yourself by being in the driver's seat. Even if you didn't help millions of people maybe you changed a life, maybe you helped just one little girl. Not bad for a day's work.

We were at a music festival and when returning to our car we walked through an area of old and custom cars. There were the old cars of course and then there was this one newer car, a Cadillac that was customized. My wife loved this car and as we looked over the changes we began to talk with the owner. He was telling us the story of how he showed up on Friday night and they allowed him to be part of the car show, but when he returned on Sunday they didn't want him to participate. His car wasn't old enough to be parked near the other old and classic cars. He offered to park away from the other cars out of respect, but his car was fully customized so it certainly was of show quality. He didn't mind obeying the rules it is just that they changed each day and he wasn't sure what they were. He certainly was not impressed with this car club that seemed to take over that part of the show. When he asked the organizers they had no problem with him participating. That club certainly didn't help themselves. As we continued talking with the owner he began to tell us about a business he wanted to start with his car. As a marketing professional I began helping him develop some ideas during the conversation.

Now my wife usually tells me afterwards that I help people too much. I don't believe you can help anyone too much unless you are doing the task for them. I just happen to be enthusiastic about helping people succeed in life because I know first hand that if you can break out of that bubble that surrounds us all and take a new idea into a different level it can make all the difference in the world. What if he succeeds, what if he becomes the next best thing because of one of my ideas? It's not like I am about to buy a car and start the same business. These were just off the cuff ideas that he can develop or not depending on the amount of work he wants to put into them. You can't make someone work with your ideas but you can make them second guess themselves to develop a better option. I just help people as I go along. As we ended out our conversation he asked for my card which I gave to him. I didn't take his card and have no intent of following up with him, if he reaches out to me then fine. This was just one person helping another in a casual conversation.

The point of this story is that you can be an ambassador for you ,your company, your club, or your industry just by helping someone without worrying about what you will get out of it. Treat people in a positive light, help when asked and promote people's well being. Those of us in the transportation industry can attest to this, go on channel 19 of the C.B. radio and ask for directions into a company in the area. Once you take out the jerks that will come on the radio with a snide remark you will get one or two people that will actually be trying to give you the right information. Now if I ask you which one are you what would be the answer, would you give the snide remarks or would you be the ambassador trying to help another person in a tough spot? Only you know the answer to that question, but I know we should all be trying to be the ambassador. That starts with helping the person next to you.

Being an ambassador is great for both you and your career, but many people feel that a little too lofty a goal, it sounds like becoming President or Prime Minister of the country. But what about a brand? When I write about business and entrepreneurship for my blogs and columns I often talk about creating a brand for yourself as your name is one of the most important parts of your identity. If you can't be trusted it doesn't matter how good you are at talking with people or how good the product or service is that your selling.

In transportation the idea is no different. Your company wants to know that you can be trusted with their thousands of dollars worth of equipment and that you can handle the freight that may be worth millions of dollars.

They also trust you will arrive at the appointed time for delivery. In other words they are putting their trust in you, in your abilities based upon previous performance. Needless to say that you have follow the rules and regulations of the road and do it in a timely manner. After all your name is at stake and integrity is everything. Don't believe me just ask any dispatcher or terminal manager who they rely on when the going gets tough, when the load has to get there without problems, when there is high dollar freight involved? It's not that driver that never arrives on time, drives like a maniac, and could care less about customer service.

It can be a double edge sword to be the good professional driver. It can be great for your career and your pocket book as you get higher profile loads, dedicated runs, are asked to move freight for larger clients and so on. With a good name in the industry it can take you along way even into the ranks of management and beyond. However there is a small downside, you get more work. Now most of us are looking for the miles so that isn't always an issue, but as you become more of a brand and someone that can be counted on you will find you are asked to do more above and beyond the call of your job.

For me I was known as the clean junkie, washing my truck before each run, keeping it looking good at all times, well that would get me working the parade route for our company. It was fun at first, but as the years went by the preparation time before the parade got shorter and shorter until one day arrived home from a run and didn't even have time to wash the truck because the company knew it would be the clean even without the wash. This happened at several companies and today I don't even like parades. This however is a small price to pay for a good name in this industry. The recognition of being a quality driver has taken my career to heights I never imagined and has opened many doors within this industry.

If you are looking at a long career in this industry then integrity is everything. It will help you create income and help you come back from setbacks. Integrity is what you do, who you are, and who you stand for, integrity is your brand. Protect it like you would your children.

When I hold workshops for professional drivers I get two types of people in the workshop. One set is very eager to have a successful career and are new to the industry, the other have been around a while and figure their career has already been set. In the workshop my main message is that what you do throughout your career follows you where ever you go. The reason for that is that is your brand. Your name is your brand and if you think of yourself as a little business you will protect that name for all it's worth. Your name is what people know you by and gives them the first impression as to the type of person you are. We all know how small the transportation industry is and names and facts get around. Some companies won't care but most decent companies won't jeopardize their record by hiring people that will tarnish their image or safety record. Your name, brand, and image are all connected which makes you either a liability or an asset, the choice is yours. The same as teenagers we don't think the things we do earlier in life will affect us later on but we all know or find out later how untrue that is. Things have a way of following us along in our lives from one place to another even if we have forgotten about them. So how do you keep your brand in top shape?

Operate in a professional manner on the job, not matter what the job. As I tell many people in my workshops for newer drivers even if you want to change positions down the road you need keep your career in check early on. Although I know people in this situation, if you want to be the safety person for a company later in your career, having a list of accidents as a driver isn't going to give you much credibility in that department, if you're still working in the industry at that point. if you want to be a dispatcher having lousy time management skills won't take you very far. Everything follows you in your career so keeping your brand clean is the best thing you can do. If your brand has been tarnished up to now then you can still make it right, correct the things that have been going wrong, learn skills and techniques that you may need to take you to the next level. Increasing your brand awareness is the best way to secure your career for the future.

Frank was new to transportation and the company. Fresh out of school he was eager to learn the ropes and have a successful career. He asked many questions almost to the point of annoyance, but what many didn't know he was watching to see the successful drivers and learn how they operated. Frank had a reason for this, his work performance had been spotty, he had a habit of always trying to fit in and usually ended up taking in the wrong information. Like the time he was told to take some time off the job to go fishing and have a colleague clock in, everyone was doing it he was told until they all got caught. As the new guy Frank got fired and this seemed to be a trend in his work history. This time would be different however, and he found a few people that showed him the right way to operate was to watch and listen. As he was getting used to the new job he noticed a beautiful truck come through the gates of the yard. As the truck pulled up to the pumps for fuel Frank went over to admire the truck and introduce himself. The two drivers started up a conversation and Frank asked how he got such a beautiful ride. "The company," replied the driver. "The company bought you a truck like that?" Frank said. "Every two or three years they bring in a few new ones," said the driver. Frank was beaming, he would love to drive one of these beautiful rigs. "What have you got to do to get one of those?" Frank asked. "Do you have to run long, stay out for days on end or anything like that?" The driver laughed and replied, "That's what everyone thinks, but the trick is increasing your worth to the company. Make yourself important to have around by operating like a true professional."

Most drivers don't think about how they work at a company. They come and go and figure the company will always need drivers not matter what they do. The truth is that a company may need those drivers, but the best thing is for them to want those drivers. That happens by making yourself so important that losing you would hurt their operation. Two things make drivers important to the company, what they know, and how they operate. A driver with experience and knowledge are extremely important to the seamless operation of a trucking company. They improve fleet performance and profit margins. The first item of importance is how a driver operates. A driver that is a safe driver, has good communication skills, a clean and neat appearance help set standards for the company, increase their professionalism to clients, and bring the operation to a place of quality. Those types of drivers are often rewarded by new equipment and incentives therefore increasing their satisfaction level while increasing their net worth to the company. The second item is knowledge, a driver that knows how to operate efficiently, can make good decisions on the road increasing a company's operation and can move a company into new markets. These drivers are often rewarded with better runs and steady freight.

If you want to remain in the top percentage of quality drivers at your company increasing your net worth is one way to do that. Here is how you may fit into the whole mix of a company.

It's hard enough these days to become a professional driver. New license regulations, procedures, and rating programs make it difficult to keep up with the industry as a whole and give you breathing room to find your footing. Add to that equation the hardship of finding a quality carrier to work for and the transportation industry can be a daunting industry to work in. For a company to be successful it has to be noted as a decent carrier following the rules yet turning a profit in very competitive industry, you have a mix that can fail at any time, and takes a great number of people working together to make it work successfully. Welcome to the world of trucking and transportation.

Think about it, have you ever worked for a company that had drivers that didn't care? Have you ever had a company that thought the way to make money was to bend the rules and work against the law? Have you ever seen a company that undercuts the rates and still can't be a successful company? Many companies have tried to be successful the wrong way. They hire people that really don't care about their careers or industry, they focus on stealing freight from someone else instead of searching out their own quality contracts. They don't care about the people they hire, they feel you are a number, not a person. There is a reason that these companies don't survive, there's a reason they can't get drivers, and there's a reason they go bankrupt. That reason is teamwork.

Culture makes or breaks a team and any quality carrier has created a culture of teamwork that flows to the very last employee hired. Teamwork starts from the top of the company and flows through the different departments within the company. You can see it, in the equipment, in the contracts, and in the drivers. A company promoting a team culture is aware that each person employed on the team is important and to be on the team you need to do your part to help make it successful.

In transportation your company chain may look like this, the President sets the goals for a quality team, the sales force looks at quality sustainable contracts, The Maintenance Supervisor buys and maintains quality equipment, the Safety Director hires only quality drivers. The drivers deliver on time and in a professional and safe manner. When this happens the company gains more business, holds a higher retention rate and can offer better working conditions. If any link in the chain doesn't do their part the company will have a hard time succeeding. So going for the gold and making your company successful starts with you, no matter where you are on the chain. Being professional is the biggest thing you can do to ensure the success of your team and get it to the gold. All of this leads down to one person in the end and that's you, the driver or Owner Operator. First impressions count

You're driving down the highway, you've just finished washing your car and a truck blows by you on the highway it is rusted, dirty, and the decal on the door is put on crooked and worn, what is the first thing that goes through your mind? If the word "Cowboy" comes to mind then you are thinking the same thing that I am, in fact if possible I would probably have moved over a lane just so the dirt doesn't fly off onto my car.

Now if I was able to read the company name on the door I have already formed an opinion of that company without even knowing anything about them. That is the mindset of one person seeing one truck. What happens if I see two or three trucks from the same company kept in the same way? That's right I am assuming that the rest of the fleet looks the same and that the company doesn't care about their image to the public. That may or may not be true depending on the people heading up the company, but there is one thing that they aren't doing is keeping an eye on the fleet while it is on the road. The same holds true if the trailer is dirty inside when you pull into a loading dock. The first thing that the shipper thinks is the whole company keeps their equipment like this, how do they drive our freight? For companies that spend thousands of dollars on advertising and sales you have just blown the company image out of the water in a matter of seconds. I have talked about this before in past columns, do you want to be the reason a company loses a major contract, and it really is up to you? So why should you bother to keep your equipment clean, why should you be the leader in your industry or company?

The reason because you are a professional, right? Professionals know more and do more than is required for a project or position. Companies try to encourage a professional image by having paint codes, inspection programs, and more but none of those things can make someone responsible every minute of the day. That takes something from inside the person themselves. Many companies spend serious dollars to make sure their drivers have a comfortable truck to call home so to see it treated badly makes everyone sad. Have you ever seen a beautiful truck that when new probably cost around $120,000 to see it look like it is on its last legs at three or four years old? Once you own or are assigned a truck it is up to you to keep that truck looking good and well maintained. What can you get out of keeping a truck in tip top shape?

The reasons are endless, but I will put a few here to help you understand the footprint you make on the industry. September has National Trucking Week and that should be a reminder to you as to the importance of what you do for the country and the public. Your image also helps a company attract like minded professional drivers to the company and sets the bar of expectation for new drivers to the industry. Your clean truck also helps the company attain new business through word of mouth from other shippers and executives in the industry. The clean truck will also help your own self image and give you that much needed boost of professionalism that you should feel as a professional driver. The last but not least is your career, the way you keep your equipment gives you longevity in your career because that is the type of driver everyone wants, pride is a major factor in how far drivers can go in their careers. So if that isn't enough for you then maybe a career as a driver is not for you. I haven't even gone into the money saved in preventative maintenance, or the respect gained through inspections on the road. Show us the professional you are by how much you care and show the public that they should be celebrating us all year long.

Most people don't realize it but your name in life is everything. In the business world companies spend millions of dollars to build their brand and market themselves as the front runner in their markets.

This is big business and a large investment for a company to make. But what about the little guy, what about you and me, how do we fit in with the whole brand thing? What is the future of our profession as a driver? Most of the public and some industry people as well lump all drivers and owner operators together in one big pool, sometimes at the expense of pushing down good people. The media has done this in the past and many companies do this to this day. Where did they get this notion, from television, from the stories of experienced dispatchers, and from us, the drivers?

We all know that one guy, he was always late, partied too hard on the road, and barely made it to his destination without some big catastrophe happening. The equipment he used was always dirty, a sight for sore eyes in front of the customers, and we won't go into the logbook part of the story. There are many drivers out there like that and unfortunately they get a lot of attention. In my experience of 25 years on the road however, that is not the norm for our industry, they just happen to have the spotlight. They are entertaining and even when they are gone or no longer involved in our industry they are remembered. That my friends is too bad because it overshadows the rest of us doing a decent days work with pride.

Many drivers and industry leaders in the past thought that was our future for the transportation sector. With all of the changes in regulations and criteria for drivers they are seeing they were wrong. We are seeing just the beginning of the changes whether we like them or not. I personally don't think the transportation industry will ever go away; we will always have goods and services to move. The mode of transportation may change and that is to be expected. The driver of the future may be driving space ships instead of trucks and vehicles and they may move on tracks instead of roads but the driver will still be needed. I do think in the future the technological side will reduce the manpower required by most companies making our industry even more specialized. Who knows how that will happen there will probably be deliveries to galaxies instead of states or provinces but that is all hearsay and yet to be seen.

There is one thing that will remain constant, one thing that what you do today will affect how people see you in the future, your name integrity. You can have a trucking career for as long as you wish in this day and age by keeping your name clear and clean. Not just on the safety side, but on the integrity side. Delivering on time, being a team player, and giving excellent customer service will all go a long way to keeping on top of a changing industry. The change is starting so I ask you, will your name be top of mind in the future of our industry, or will you remain in the shadows? When the pressure is on is when leadership really starts.

It was one of the most important games in history in a sport that is known for it's passion and turmoil. The stakes were high, as this was the Olympics. Unless you had your head buried in the sand as of late you would know about the controversial soccer game between Canada and the United States where the referee of the game made a rare call that is perceived to have taken the game away from the Canadian team.

Now I am not here to make any judgments on the call itself or the players or referee in focus of the now FIFA investigation. I am here to bring to light how easy a passionate situation can get out of hand for all of us if we don't do our best to keep conditions calm. In this case the comments caught on camera seem to be weighing in at the same amount to the call made by the referee in the game. Even in junior play there have been battles in the heat of the moment between fathers, coaches, and so on. That's where the trouble begins. I am sure this has happened to all of us, in 25 years of trucking I have seen all kinds of things happen at scales, when given a ticket for something wrong with the truck that doesn't make sense. What about the height of frustration when people don't stand behind their products or services?

We have all experienced this at one time or another in as many situations as you can make up. Whether family, friends, or external sources this is time when leadership needs to be forefront and centre. Should you say something to an officer inspecting your truck if you find an incorrect inspection? Yes! Should the Captain or Coach of team in question state their case? Absolutely! It's how you do it that makes the difference, getting into a screaming match with the person of authority will rarely get you out of the hot seat. As each person gets their back up the situation will deteriorate more and more until a charge is laid that can't be reversed. Just look at any domestic case to get proof of these types of situations. How many drivers have tried to argue it out at the scales with an officer and found a few more tickets added on to the first one. We have all been there. Heck, I have even lost it one time when I bought a new phone, needed help after the purchase and found the dealer unwilling to help me. I went through their corporate stores, called the software company among others to get nowhere. Now stuck with piece of metal for two years it took two months before I was able to get it working and had nothing but problems for the rest of my contract. Don't think I didn't let go on the person I bought it from, that's pure frustration. Did I exude leadership no way. Had that scenario been on the street I may be in jail. I've learned that nothing beneficial comes out of that.

If you find yourself in those types of situations, then realize that keeping calm is the first part of leadership. Once you have done that clearly state your case and make sure notes are taken that you don't agree with the judgment. Then either fight it in a professional environment through the proper channels, leave it alone, or find some other professional way of dealing with the situation. I have found this to work the best, it may take longer, but it will be more beneficial than letting loose on the scene. In the heat of the battle leadership starts when the pressure's on.

It is very hard for leadership to just happen, many times it is built up over time and based on your value system. Over the last few months there has been a big story in the media regarding a family that killed their two girls and the husband's ex-wife. The family being accused and recently found guilty had said they did the horrific deed because their daughters were, shall we say being absorbed in western culture. This case got me thinking to how far would you go to protect your honor, integrity, or any other leadership quality you feel to be important? Now I certainly am not suggesting that anybody commit murder to protect any of those qualities as that would take you back to the other side of the leadership track. However there must be some internal setting within a person that makes them stand up for honesty, integrity, and the honor of their name? If there wasn't then we would all be criminals without a care of the consequence of our actions.

As a leadership coach and consultant and someone whose whole life has been built on my name integrity is high on my list of items that I keep dear to my heart. Like most people I don't impose my idea of honor onto others, but set the standards in myself and don't drop below the line. This internal setting is developed based on values that are important to me and my family name. For many people that bar is hard to set, it is also hard to keep at that level over time. I remember struggling with the right and wrong thing when I was a kid. Have you ever done that? For instance my parents taught me that on a bus or public transit you are to give up your seat to an older person, someone who is pregnant, etc. This caused great turmoil as in those days it wasn't cool to do ,that is why we sat in the back. My friends weren't brought up the same way therefore I was always questioned for doing it.

I used to always be judging people as to were they old enough to stand or did they have to sit, would they make it all the way to the back of the bus and so on? It was very stressful! Holding the door was the same thing, when I am at a mall my wife thinks I am the doorman as I never get to go through it. Today I am glad the way I was brought up, but at times it has been a challenge.

So the point of this story is how important are your values to you? Are you trying to fit in with the crowd and do what they do or are you willing to stand on your own for your values and your name? There is only one person that has that answer and if you look in the mirror you will find that person.

This is why I have found the best way to be successful in trucking is to play by your own set of rules. Have you ever watched the careers of different individuals and wondered why some succeed and are profitable and others always seem to be struggling? I see it over and over again in my travels and always wonder what makes some people tick and others lose out. Now there is two mindsets to this thought process; some say it doesn't matter how you finish as long as you finish first, and others say it is best to finish second and ethically than to be first through cheating. I agree with the second thought process. Here is why, most criminals get caught sooner or later, and those types of people spend too much energy trying to beat the system rather than working within it. Now this article is not about becoming a criminal, but about steering your career by abiding by the rules of engagement. Let me share a story with you and you may recognize a person like this on your team. Now this story is based in the transportation industry but you can find similar examples in almost any industry. By the way I have changed the names to protect the guilty.

Let's call this person Jack, he has been driving truck his whole life. He learned to drive from his father and the family has a long list of truck drivers in it. He was taught early on that the most important part of creating money as a truck driver is to put in as many miles as you can, no matter how you do it drive those miles under your belt. Jack succeeded at that and companies loved him because he would do anything they asked, run around the scale, driver over the allowable hours, and take heavy loads whenever asked. With that attitude it was no problem to get jobs and he always seemed to be working. There was one problem however; he didn't care about his career. As long as he was making money he didn't give another thought as to how to proceed to the next step. Due to his non caring attitude Jack did a lot of damage to equipment, refused to go that extra mile by keeping his truck clean and would eventually be fired.

He only had one goal and that was to get on with a good company that paid well and even though he bounced around companies he finally got that chance and ended up with a great company. The problem was that the mindset he had created early on never left him and while trying to make that extra dollar again he ended up rolling the truck. He made it out alive however; he has a hard time finding decent companies to work for and will never find that gold mine that he once worked at again.

Now Tom on the other hand did not come from a long line of truck drivers, but a line of accountants. He started at the bottom of the industry moving furniture and gradually through hard work, passion for his positions, and putting extra effort into his career, moved up the ladder getting experience in various industries within the transportation sector.

In the long run he made better money than his counterpart Jack by abiding by company rules, putting in extra effort, and looking for opportunities to do what he loves to do. How did he make more money than Jack you ask? He worked for better companies that paid more per mile, he achieved higher positions that paid in various ways such as salary or percentage that created more income than by the mile, and he kept his record clean giving him a good name in the industry. He has since gone onto other avenues and opportunities within the transportation industry.

Now I tell you that story so that you will look hard at your career in the past, present, and future to decide if it is taking you on the path you had hoped it would. Part of the reason people go down the wrong path is due to the fact that they listen to the wrong people regarding their career. I myself was told over thirty years ago not to get into the industry because you couldn't make any money in it. Thank the Lord I didn't listen to that guy or I would still be pumping gas at the local gas station. Owning your success is about believing in your own ways of doing things that make you unique while abiding by the rules and regulations of your industry. Sometimes money grows on trees so think of your career as the trunk and branches. But what about the smaller picture of being successful with the carrier you're with. Maybe it is a matter of feeling safe, or traveling in certain areas, how do your own rules fit in here?

John was a brand new driver, he had only been driving a month and was scared to death of going to the East Coast. Until now he had been running mostly Midwest without too much trouble. He had heard the stories of places like Hunts Point Market in New York and cities like the Bronx. The company he ran for however operated within 500 miles of his home terminal so he knew at some point he would be asked to go to that part of the country. He spent another few weeks running Midwest and then it happened, he was asked to go east. As the load came out the window from dispatch he read it and almost fainted, Long Island was the town noted on the paperwork. Long Island, how would he get to Long Island? He had two choices to make, he could refuse the load or he could take it and make the best of it. After a moment of thinking John decided to refuse the load, and therefore was put back at the bottom of the dispatch log. It would mean another half day waiting for another load to come his way.

This happens to many drivers and owner operators who have heard stories from other drivers about traveling the East Coast. The stories are so bad they scare the crap out of anyone who even listens to them. Unfortunately too many guys believe the stories and find out too late that the story wasn't as bad as first explained. All the reasons are usually stated like traffic, crime, tight corners, expensive tolls, and rude people. I'll agree that many of those issues can be found in the city, but those issues can be found in any big city across North America, or the world for that matter. Show me a city that doesn't have traffic, crime, tight corners, and expensive tolls, or rude people. You will never get away from that and even running Midwest you will find those problems in Chicago, Indianapolis, and other cities. It's how you handle them that make you a professional driver. Refusing work based on a story you heard, or because you believe it may be a bad place is a waste of time. You will only hurt yourself in the long run as you won't be perceived as a team player, your financial picture will suffer as you spend much of your running time waiting for loads, and you will always be afraid of that area of the country.

The solution to the problem is to run by your own rules and be good at what you do. The thin line is to make sure you know why you are running this way and to be consistent. This isn't just a way to get out of work, this is a way to keep you in work. For instance when I used to run New York City and the East Coast I made up rules that I would stick to. I wouldn't refuse a load to the East Coast but would have provisions such as if I didn't feel safe sleeping in that area I would pull the truck out to an area I felt safe. I would go back in the next day if I had to. This put the pressure on dispatch to think about my back haul ahead of time, and if I did pull the truck out of that area I would get paid for my miles. Many times I got my return load before even leaving for the trip. You will find dispatch is happy to have anyone go to the East Coast. Study the area for yourself, know your equipment and what it can do. My other rule is the 40 mile an hour rule. I use this one for bad weather, but if I can't do at least 40 miles an hour then I am best to find a truck stop to stop in and wait for the weather or road conditions to clear up. If this puts you late to a customer you need to back yourself up by being able to explain why you were late. The secret to running by your own rules is communication and a willingness to get the job done. Many times you can make better money running the East Coast so refusing work in this area is foolish. Since most companies run in this areas there is lots of work there, if you want miles then that is the area for you.

To run these areas or anywhere for that matter certain soft skills and values are required to make it. Values like patience, honesty, and respect are all required in this industry to make it successfully.

They say "patience is a virtue!" and even though I have been searching for "They" my whole life they may be right. Have you ever seen that lady just lose it over a coupon in line at the grocery store? Have you ever sat in a receiving line at a large distribution warehouse waiting to be unloaded? How about the scale guard that pulls you over for nothing but the time of day you crossed the scale and decides to train the new inspector? An hour later your patience level may be wearing very thin. In the transportation industry patience is not only a virtue, but a requirement. Think about this for a minute, in one trip a driver can be delayed in so many ways. Let's say you start your day and the truck won't start, then you leave and you're in the heart of traffic, a couple of hours later you are stopped for an inspection at the scale, and then you finally get to your destination to find you have to wait three hours to be unloaded. Welcome to the normal day of a professional truck driver

How do you battle those types of delays so that you are not ready to walk away from the truck and job all together? Patience is one way, you must have a high level of it. Some drivers find that out early in their career and others find it out late in their careers. Just having a high level of patience will not solve the whole problem however, other factors play a part in the process.

One of those factors is your composure level. Like that women at the checkout some people fly off the handle at the littlest incident and enjoy creating a scene. That is their make up, they don't think twice about it or how it affects anyone else. We can find examples of those type of people all over the world. The other factor is planning. You as a professional driver are in a position through experience to look at all the possible delays and obstacles that you may come across on your trip. By planning to avoid or handle those elements that may delay you is the first way to combat obstacles on the road.

Once you have evaluated the type of person you are and have planned for those obvious delays you have one more factor to take into account. The third factor is to "let go" and do your best. You can't control what everyone else does, you can only control your own actions. If you have done everything in your power to avoid delays, you have learned to handle your composure when problems happen, and you have realized you have done all you can do, then you have done your job. You can't be held at fault for issues out of your control. Realizing that gives you piece of mind. Realizing that helps you stay calm and in control. Realizing that makes you the professional driver that you are. Patience is a virtue, it's also a requirement! Get yours in check!

But what about honesty? This is an areas that I have seen compromised by even the best of us. Things can go wrong and honesty can get you through whether it is the mysterious damage on the truck or lying on your resume. Things today are quite different from what they were years ago in the transportation industry. For instance more items are going electronic, you now have to be a smart cookie to handle a big rig and keep up on all the regulations for being in compliance, but some people for whatever reason just don't seem to get it when they start on with a new company. Nowadays they have a way to test for much of the practical knowledge required for the position of commercial driver, but some companies are still taking your word that you know what you are doing.

You know what I am talking about, the guy who comes in to the job claiming he has done it all under the sun from flatbed to reefer, and steel, but is only 22 years old. The guy who feels he is too cool to listen to the trainer and doesn't listen to the instructions in case something new is required when loading. There are many of these types out there and I have seen many come and go in my time at the wheel. If you watch them closely you will find that they don't really know what they are doing and usually will screw up with a load in a very short time because they didn't listen when being told how to do the job. That is why so many companies have started training programs so people won't get into trouble in there first few weeks of employment. Those are the people that give the industry a bad name and I am not saying that things can't happen but as a professional driver it is your job to make sure that you have done everything to the best of your abilities in securing your load or operating in a safe manner.

So what is the best course of action to making sure you are working at your best. The first part is to know what you should be doing, know the regulations, and have the proper equipment to get the job done. Be organized, this is a big one with me, you have to keep an eye on your equipment and know what is becoming too worn to do the job and what is ready for replacing. Being organized not only helps you track your equipment but also makes you look much more professional in front of the shippers and receivers. Have you ever seen a driver that looked like he had to unload his truck before beginning to load because he kept it such a mess, I have? If you are required to use a certain amount of straps for your load, but feel it would be safer with an extra one go ahead and use it. I have never seen anyone given a ticket for going beyond the regulations to be safe. The same thing goes for checking your load, if getting that load down the road safely requires that you stop a little bit more to make sure it is safe then do that. It doesn't matter if you are only required to stop once. Leadership means stepping up to the plate and being a professional can mean the difference between saving lives and staying employed.

Our industry in general has been trying to get respect from the general public for as long as I can remember. This is partially due to the way many drivers in the early days got their jobs as drivers and that continued into the 90's and in some regards is still a factor today. We have passed this model down through our kids by telling them to get an education and get a decent job. Our society in general doesn't regard truck drivers as a skill to be taken seriously, so of course we have no respect. My question to you is, why? I don't understand how a person can drive a truck in an industry for years themselves and then tell everyone else to go and do something else! If you don't like the job then go do something else, if you like the profession then why not share that with others. If you don't respect yourself then no one else will.

Respect comes right down to the way you operate on a day to day basis. If you think that you are just another stupid truck driver then you are telling yourself that you are not as good as the next person and we all know that is not true. Those of you in the industry know how hard it is to do this job, and the information you need to know most people don't comprehend. Go ahead, next time you sit down with your friends and family start telling them about hours of service regulations, distributing the weight properly on a trailer to run legal, or the science behind specking a trailer with 10'-1' spread. If they are still sitting there when you finish they will be amazed, if they have left then they don't feel adequate because they don't understand any of that. You have to be a smart cookie to be a truck driver in this day and age and has been shown in many statistics the weak don't make it for long. Respect is so important that it translates into everything you do. So what is the secret to gaining more of it and being seen as a world class operator?

The secret is you! How you deal with people on a day to day basis, the way you think about yourself, the way you operate all create respect for yourself and how others see you as a professional driver. You probably think I am asking you to be a saint, but that is not true. Trust me there were many days when I wanted to strangle the person on the other side of the dispatch window, or at least give them that look that tells them they are not as big as they think they are. The truth is it is harder to be the bigger person and sometimes biting your tongue can be the best thing you can do for your career.

Sometimes people are just having a bad day. If you have done everything to the best of your abilities, operated as a true professional, and completed your job the way it should be done then you will gain the respect of your coworkers and more importantly the respect of yourself. Respect comes from within and it doesn't matter if anyone told you how good a job you did, the point is that you know you did a good job. If you see a co-worker having trouble give them a helping hand, everyone was new once. Think of it this way, everyone has heard of the phrase "he would give you the shirt off his back" now nowhere in that phrase does it say how smart a person is, but the person repeating it has total respect for the person they are talking about. That my friend is the way most of us would want to be thought of in a conversation where we are not present. So if you haven't been getting the respect you deserve, have you been giving it? So I ask where are you parked on the street of respect?

Step 4

Choosing a Carrier

Wohen you're in a program or school situation your whole goal is to get that license and get going in your new career. For those going through a second career type of program it may be a whole new industry for you. Possibly some of you have friends or family that have worked in transportation and you plan to follow in their footsteps. If you don't have that insider information on how to choose a carrier to work for, it can be very intimidating to the newcomer. The talk of miles, money per mile, sign on incentives, family time, road time, experience, it goes on and on. Learning the lingo can be a problem all by itself so having some information before you head out on the journey of looking for a job may be the best use of time for someone. So as a new driver to the industry what do you look for, how do you evaluate who is the best carrier for you. In transportation looking for a job is not the same as looking for a job in manufacturing, or retail or other industries. You don't evaluate the job by how much they pay you an hour, what benefits you will receive after three months, or how much vacation time you will get. Those are all important but they aren't in the forefront as some of the other issues that you will have to deal with. In my first job at a fast food restaurant I don't remember asking the Manager what their policy was on waiting time. That question comes above benefits in the transportation industry.

Your very first question should be, "What type of lifestyle do I want for my career?" Why ask that question first? Trucking is a lifestyle, it doesn't shut off at 5:00pm, it doesn't have sick days, and weekends sometimes come in the middle of the week. You should be thinking of where you want to go and how long you are willing to be out on the road. This is the major point and should be discussed with your family. Do you need to be home every weekend, do you need to be home on Tuesdays? Maybe you are single and don't care where you go,that's great it gives you more opportunities. Once you have answered these questions you can start looking at the carriers that fit that bill. If you want to run California then look at carriers that go to that area. The only way you will be happy in this industry is to find the type of work you want to do and try to work there. As they say if you enjoy your work it won't feel like work. On the other hand if you want to be home each night and you sign on with a carrier that runs California you will not be happy and either will your family. Doing your homework up front is the best way to have a successful career in the transportation industry. Matching it with your lifestyle should be the first issue to look into.

At a seminar for new professional drivers it was mentioned that people becoming owner operators may have trouble finding work. Unfortunately, the information was not only incorrect but very old. I will agree that the last couple of years have been devastating to the transportation industry and many carriers were not only, not hiring new drivers, but were even laying off some. That is unusual for the industry as due to turnover rates getting drivers is normally a company's prime objective. However the economy did take a hit and the industry changed. That is in the past however and the industry is starting to make a climb back to the forefront. In fact the opposite is happening and a driver shortage is on the way.

So as a new driver or owner operator how should you know if your job will be secure? Hopefully any company wanting to hire you will have the workload to support the hire as there is a great cost to the company in hiring drivers. The one thing you could do is ask. If you come right out and ask the recruiter can you tell me for sure that I will get at least 2500 miles a week, and they answer yes, then you're good. If they aren't sure I would clear that up right away. You can make money at any company as long as the work is there. The rest is up to you and how you perform. Most companies I know will do their part if you'll do yours. When they're interviewing you, you interview them, it's a two way street.

It seems like a silly question doesn't it? Being unemployed because of the truck you are asked to drive. Most people would laugh at the statement and tell me I was lying, but the statement is closer to the truth than you know. Deep down anyone who has driven a truck understands the importance of decent equipment. In the thirty years I have been involved with the transportation industry I can understand how important the truck is, why I am one of the biggest chrome junkies around. However when looking for work there is a line as to how picky you can be, or is there?

To many the truck is a number, "We have 80 pieces of equipment in our fleet." To some it is a statement, "I only drive large cars." To others it is about name brand or quality. Now as someone who talks with drivers and Owner Operators on a regular basis I have had some drivers who will only work at a company that has Volvo Trucks. I have had potential Owner Operators suggest that they just want a shiny truck and bounce down the road and get paid. I have also had Owner Operators who believe that one make gets better fuel mileage than the other. Now I am not disputing the facts one way or the other, I am just restating what I have heard. The fact is that many times the decision on the type of truck to drive comes from previous experience, culture, and hearsay. I find many people drive Volvo trucks because that is the name that they feel comfortable with. There is nothing wrong with the trucks I used to drive them myself. I can also understand the person that likes the shiny truck as I drove Peterbilts for much of my career. These days if you are in a position to choose the company you work for then go ahead and drive for the one that has the trucks you want. That being said that kind of philosophy may have you working for companies that don't fit the type of work you are willing to do. I remember I used to do a little bit of the same type of judgment when investigating companies. I would go look at their yard and check out their equipment, if I liked what I saw, I applied. If I didn't then I moved on. My thinking was that if they kept their trucks in decent shape then it would be a good company to work for. If all the trucks looked like crap then maintenance wasn't their top priority.

Trucks come with a variety of options these days so it shouldn't be hard to get the motor and set up you want. My advice to those that are looking for work in the industry look at the merits of the company you are investigating, not the equipment they buy. The company culture is the important thing. In time you will have the equipment you wish for.

You've probably read them in the trade magazines, you know the ones, the ones that report on how good a company is to work for. I've read them many times and know of many of the companies that they talk about. Business is hard and hats off to any company that gets a mentioned in those reports, you must be doing something right and it is a long hard battle to reach the top. Many times though the reporting structure is based on a variety of positions and people in the company and information received in ballots and so on. So you can take all of those factors into account before weighing the truth or you can work from your own criteria. Often you will find that the fleets mentioned have different types of operations and are really not competing against anyone but themselves. Now I am not judging the facts or asking for recounts or any such things. I just bring this up to ask you one simple question and the only answer that matters is yours. What do you think of your company as far as a place of employment?

Why did I ask you this? I asked you this to get your thought process going about your career. The only person that can answer that is you and you should be the only person that matters from your career standpoint. So how do you like where you work? First remember this is not a perfect world, and how people rate where they are will be different for everyone. For me a good company to drive for is a place where they give you steady miles with little wait time, good quality customers that understand the importance of a quality carrier, clean well maintained equipment, operational staff that has been in the driver's seat and understands the frustrations and importance of the position. Finally you want a carrier that cares about their employees and their families. If there was a death in your family and you had to get home from a location 1000 miles away, how would they do that, would they expect you to return home on your own in due time, or would they put you on the first plane back home and take care of the truck later? If you can answer positively to these questions then you probably work for a good carrier and should be happy they treat you well. Every driver should do their own driver evaluation every couple of years to make sure the carrier you work for is meeting the career goals you have set for yourself. This will help keep yourself working towards your own goals and not be swallowed up by day to day operations of a normal truck driver.

Have you ever talked with a driver who has seen it all, "Been there done that!" You wonder as you talk with them why they have jumped from one job to another job so many times if they have all the knowledge they say they do? In our industry this happens a lot and recruiters have a nose for noticing track records like this when reviewing applicants for new positions. One of the worst things you can do is to jump from company to company making your employment record very unstable. This shows a lack of integrity to an employer and they will always be sitting on their seats wondering if you are going to leave at the drop of a hat. With the recruiting shortage upon us it is also creating a volatile market as companies are all trying to find drivers from the same driver pool. As you read those trucking magazines you will see many opportunities that look inviting, but are they really?

The grass always looks greener on the other side of the fence, but many times sends you in the dirt. The promise of more miles, lucrative sign on bonuses and much more may be tempting and urging you to make a change. Before you make that jump you will need to focus on what you have at the company where you work now and how much you will gain with a change. Only you know whether that position at the other employer is worth taking because it has to be based upon the goals you have set out for your career. If you don't know what you want from your life, how will you know if the new company can provide it to you? I have seen Owner Operators change companies to gain two cents per mile, but lose five cents a mile because they don't run their truck as a proper business model. I have also seen drivers change companies based on mileage pay alone to find out you never return home again. This happened to me when I went from a family owned operation to one of the big carriers. I was supposed to operate locally as that was where I was trying get to in my career, a little more home time with my children. The opposite happened and I ended up not coming home for a month each time I went out. After six months I went back to that family owned carrier.

Most drivers if they take a really good look around will find their current carrier is just as good as the next. If they treat you right with decent equipment, good runs, and good money then stay where you are. The only time you should really think about a change is if it is a major benefit to your career such as operation type, location, or personal experience. Make sure to investigate the operation of a company, if they pay you more money, but you end up sitting more then you are no further ahead of the game. Doing your homework will probably show you that staying where you are is the best place to be.

They were new, they were told they could make big money running a different type of freight. The miles would be the same, the countryside would be the same said the recruiter,"you won't even know the difference." The team left a viable carrier looking only at the numbers of the new carrier and what they pay. Running California was the easy part, they had a regularly scheduled run with the old carrier. They were hauling less than they thought with many partial loads with the new carrier and were on the open board, but it looked on paper as though they would make much more money hauling specialized freight. A rosy story that has turned out not to be so. What they found when switching companies was a different story. The freight they were to specialize in was very cumbersome to work with, it caused waiting time to be increased, quality control was more involved, and associated costs went up. There were even some costs that were not shown directly when calculating the transition from one carrier to another. At the end of the day the mileage pay was better but the money made was not the same.

Recently a carrier I deal with had the same issue. A team of theirs started with the company and after a couple of years thought they could make more money elsewhere. They left the carrier to run produce for another carrier because they saw dollar signs and big profits. What they didn't count on was the associated costs with that type of freight, the downtime associated with loading and unloading at terminals, and having to buy equipment that requires high maintenance. Even though they were being paid more, they were making less in the long run. The team was smart enough to realize this wasn't the type of freight that they wanted to haul and was able to get back in with their original carrier.

When evaluating carriers it is very important that you know all the details of what you will be hauling and costs associated with that. What this team found out was that in that terrific freight rate they were getting, was that they supplied their own trailer, down time was not paid, costs of fuel were higher because they hauled refrigerated product, and they sat more due to the nature of the produce industry. All these costs have to be figured out ahead of time and many may not be apparent until you have started working at the company. Speaking with someone already doing that job or a consultant that knows the industry may have saved them much time and grief. It was lucky this young team were able to rekindle the romance of their old company.

We have all done it at one time or another, either thought of changing carriers or actually went for the gold and changed. I have done it in my career and you may have done it in yours. The grass always looks greener on the other side of the fence especially days when things are going so well. Someone in the office comes down on you, the customer is having a panic attack, and you're being laid over again. These things can make you think it will be better to work over at the other place. So you make the move.

You now are over at the other carrier of choice, you have been there for a few months and find out they have the same clientele and problems that the original carrier did. Although you were promised the moon the same crap is happening with the new carrier as it did at the old carrier or worse. This happened to me when I left a carrier I had been with for three years to explore an opportunity as an Owner Operator. I was used to being home regularly on weekends at some point as my major area for driving was 500 to 1500 miles from our terminal. Many opportunities for miles, however I wanted to be home even more when my kids were born and was told I would be my own boss running city and regional only. The company hadn't thoroughly thought out the program so while they were ironing out the specifics they put me on their open board. That open board consisted of the East Coast, United States, and Ontario, Quebec. That doesn't count the creative dispatch I encountered or that trip to Newfoundland. Nothing was originally mentioned about me taking a boat to P.E.I. once a week with a few other drivers to load potatoes either, since there was no fancy bridge back then. So after six months of not being home for a month at a time I decided to go back to the carrier I had left.

Now if you have done the same thing that I have, you can go back and have a successful career. I did stay with them for a few more years before moving on to other opportunities. The major point on leaving is to do it gracefully. Don't give the boss the finger, throw your logbooks at the receptionist yelling, "You fill them out" or anything like that. You never know what will happen in life and you may run into these people again. The important part though is if you're returning is to see if you changed inside. The company most likely hasn't changed, so you have to change your mindset. Go in with a new attitude, maybe you were getting upset over things that no one can control, maybe you were the problem. Look at what went wrong, talk to the Manager and discuss how things will be different, and realize many carriers have the same problems. If you work with one that treats you right, stay!

On the next few pages I thought it would be good to take a look at some of the industries within an industry that you may find yourself working in down the road. All have good and bad elements about them and should be reviewed very carefully before diving in as an Owner Operator. Some may be completely out of reach if you are new to the industry and need a few years of experience under your belt before being accepted.

"Hazmat" for all you new to trucking is short for hazardous materials, which can include anything from cleaning fluids to gasoline, to dynamite and everything in between. It is not for the faint of heart and certainly is not for those of you that don't have good organizational skills or an eye for detail. Many carriers don't even deal with hazardous materials because the details, training, and insurance make it not worthwhile to do so. The carriers that do haul hazmat do it all the time and many times specialize in certain forms of it.

So what type of person gets into hauling this type of freight and why? First you are looking at the true professional driver if going this route. Companies don't need someone who will be a cowboy causing accidents. When a hazmat load gets into an accident the repercussions can be disastrous. Drivers in this area have attention to detail, run by the rules, and have lots of patience. Cleanliness and accuracy in paperwork is a necessity, one slip here can cause large fines from the Ministry of Transportation plus possibly the Ministry of the Environment among other agencies. The training to remain compliant is brutal and changes with each company. Companies range from anything such as consumer commodities which are not labeled to chemical transfer carriers. With many of the regulations many drivers don't even want to deal with hazmat items. There is a reason you should be looking at those types of carriers however, wages and lifestyle. You won't get into these types of carrier right off the bat, but they can be very lucrative down the road, especially if you get in the right one. Usually you will get a higher rate of pay at hazmat carrier, the equipment is usually better, and you will find them much more willing to stick to running legal.

So how do you get into these carriers? First of all keep your nose clean, and when I say that I mean both license and image. As mentioned before they don't need the cowboy mentality at work here. Operate professionally right out of the gate, investigate the carriers of your choice and find out what they need in terms of experience and training. If you can get training on your own great, or better yet start working for carriers that work with hazmat materials and learn about the regulations and types of freight available. This will give you a good base of understanding as to what needs to be on paperwork, the classes of dangerous goods, and safety points. Success in a career in transportation comes from a good attitude, a want to learn, and be willing to listen. Add hard work and you will have career of success.

One of the areas that are rarely talked about in transportation is the moving industry. A very large part of the industry as a whole, however I never hear it mentioned in training schools, nor do I see it advertised in many magazines in the transportation industry. I certainly can't be the only one that has worked in the market as millions work there and some of the largest companies around are at the forefront of the market. I am sure you have heard of them, United Van Lines, Allied Moving and Storage, Atlas Van Lines, and there are a host of others large and small. So why are they not mentioned? It may be partly due to the seasonal nature of the work, it may be due to the lifting and manual labour required to do the job, or it may be due to the lower wages at the entry level. What most people don't understand about the moving industry it can be one of the best places to learn about becoming a professional driver, and one of the best entry level opportunities for new drivers.

I started my career in the moving industry, mostly by accident really. I just needed a job at 17 and humping furniture as we called it was what came up. I had no license except my "G" license at the time and no experience at all with the trucking industry. I spent five years in the moving side of life from helper to Owner Operator before moving into the freight side of the industry. There is one key factor that made it a great learning ground, dealing with the public. Due to the fact you are dealing with the public you will learn the essential tools for a successful career in transportation. You will learn time management, customer service skills, cleanliness, attention to detail, time and distance estimating, hiring practices, teamwork, lifting techniques, and unique driving skills. This is training you won't find anywhere else, but what about the money? The money is good and bad depending on how you look at it. You will probably start at an hourly rate when starting but there are many opportunities to make more money. Most highway loads are paid on percentage, so the better you are at watching expenses the more money you can make. The better you are at packing the truck, the more money you can make. Thinking long term in the business is very beneficial because things can move fast for the good worker. Drivers are the leaders of the team and decide how things should be done so having people skills can be a great asset. The industry has taught me a lot and it can be a great starting point to a long career for those that don't mind some hard work. So what should your first steps be to getting into the industry?

Learn more about it, talk to people who do it for a living. Talk with other drivers about their experience and make appointments to visit carriers in the business. You may find a gold mine of opportunity that is never talked about.

They criss cross this country bringing us our most precious commodity, food! Without them the grocery shelves would be empty, the stores would close, and your dining table would look really bare at your next meal. Most drivers hauling produce make great money, but it takes a certain type of temperament to be successful in this part of the transport industry. The reason they are called "Chicken Haulers" is that in the old days most of the drivers had really fancy equipment because the demand for their work kept them moving all the time. Everyone needs food. As they ran most of the night to get product on the shelves they outlined their trucks with many lights that became known as Chicken Lights. With shiny rigs, fancy lights, and product in demand it can create an illusion of fantasy for those looking at work options in the transportation industry.

The truth is that while many do well in the produce area there are many that fail and fail terribly. While the money may look good you have to weigh the pros and cons of the industry. Getting paid double what many other drivers are getting paid is one thing, but waiting time in this sector is extremely long. You can wait from hours to days without pay and then when loaded will be expected to run and deliver in a rush. You have many more things to worry about such as temperature maintenance, trailer washouts after certain loads, quality checks at border crossings, and long lineups at major receiving terminals. Many times you will be expected to not only have your own truck but be willing to provide a trailer unit as well. Costs add up in this area when you add on wash outs, additional fuel consumption for the refrigeration unit, and additional costs on the road. This industry can be very cut throat if you don't know what you're doing. It takes a strong person to be successful here.

So if you are still interested in getting onto this part of the industry then you will need certain things in order to make it. Patience is the first mandatory item, be prepared to wait at each end for large terminals. Know all your costs up front and have a solid business plan if you plan on owning your own equipment in this industry. If you will be just a driver you will probably need a couple of years experience to qualify at most companies. If you go to work for a company try to work for a company that specializes in produce and has quality equipment. Again this industry isn't for the faint of heart, you have to know your stuff to survive, the weak get eaten alive.

Okay so you're like the rest of us, you're star struck! You want to haul real cool freight, not just those muddy tractors, but real star quality material. Maybe your dream is to haul for your favourite band, or lead the transportation team on a wild tour from city to city? Maybe your dream is to haul in the race circuit where you will help your team win the top trophy one track at a time? We all dream like that and for many of us it remains a dream. Most of my life my dream was to drive a coach for a group on tour, I used to love the fancy buses, I still do, but that dream got dipped in reality. I had a friend that had a band and I have been waiting for him to make it big to fulfill that dream, but since he has taken a different career path it is still a dream. For many this can be a reality!

Many of us think that those rock and roll stars have so much money that they just buy their own fleet of trucks and go on tour whenever they want, but that is not usually the case. There are a few companies that handle tours and other types of special events and do it well. For most people especially new drivers, while the glitz and glamour of working for the stars is alluring there is a price to pay and that price may not be worth the personal stake most people are willing to pay. For instance are you willing to be gone from home for days to weeks to months in some cases while on tour? Once a tour is set it may be on the road for a long time. This is even more important if you get into a race track scenario like NASCAR. That race circuit is set and has many people involved and as a driver you are an important element of that team. These are important parts of the show circuit that many don't think about. Getting past the shiny truck is the important part, you may not even see the stars as you will be dealing with the road manager.

So what type of person goes down this route of being a driver to the stars? First you must have a passion for the job, this is not for someone that doesn't care about freight handling and cleanliness. You should have good time management skills, and be good at following directions. Most places won't be looking at new drivers so you can expect to need two to five years of experience before landing these types of jobs. Driver professionalism is key here and those that don't fit the bill won't make the grade. Flexibility in schedule is also required. Are you willing to be gone for long periods of time, what if a show gets held over? If Lady Gaga gets a cold and holds the performance up what happens the to the drivers? If you are interested in going this route as a professional driver, keep your nose clean and work hard. It may seem like a far shot, but willingness and investigation into the companies in that area of the industry will give you the right footing into working with the stars.

Step 5

Setting Up Your Business

Y ou've heard me talk in the past about stepping up to the plate when you're going into business for yourself. In fact I think you should step up to the plate when becoming a professional driver in general. Just when you think people are starting to get it I read an article or hear a story about how foolish people can be. I just finished reading an article on how to dress and operate when going through a road test and interview at a company that again was going over the basics of how to dress, and how to act. Have we not beat that horse to death already, have people not got the message? Apparently not or we wouldn't be talking about it. The same thing happens in business, eventually you have to get the message. Eventually you have to decide if you are going to be in business or be a statistic for failure. Now before I get all kinds of comments I realize that businesses fail for much more reasons than not operating business like or taking themselves too seriously. Those aren't the businesses I am talking about here. There are many factors that determine if a business stays profitable or not. That being said I do believe that through an entrepreneurial view and Owner Operator standpoint many people getting into business today take it seriously until they have to do the work. So what am I getting at here?

Evaluation, operation, and dedication are the keys to success as a business owner or Owner Operator. For those of you that are new Owner Operators you will get good and bad information on the industry, certain companies, and the life of an Owner Operator from others. That advice however may not be from sources that are interested in seeing you succeed in this industry. To succeed in this industry and be one of the successful instead of one of the statistics takes working with the keys of a successful operation. The three keys listed above if used correctly will go along way to helping you have a successful business whether it be as an Owner Operator or other business arrangement.

Evaluation is the first one however these aren't in any particular order. Evaluation of your business is the key to creating a successful business. I remember when I started out in business I thought I was on the right track, but the drive for success, and the will to take on some risks for rewards down the road kept me evaluating each success and failure. The failures were turned around as learning curves and either revised or trashed so they will never happen again. As I look back down the road if I hadn't been evaluating my business, if I hadn't kept pushing the envelope for new opportunities we wouldn't be in business today. It is important to keep your eye on the big picture.

Operation is an area that many people get lost in especially Owner Operators and entrepreneurs. They get overwhelmed in the many tasks and duties expected of them and end up doing all of them badly or some not at all. Bookkeeping and taxes come to mind in this area. You need to keep fine-tuning your operation, making sure the important areas are being taken care of by qualified people not just someone looking to make an extra buck. It is vital that you keep evaluating what works and how to make your operation run smoothly. Go through a tax audit and you will quickly learn what information is required.

Dedication is the final key and when you signed on the dotted line, or you left your job to open a business, or you decided to make this your life's work, you went into dedication mode. Be dedicated to being successful in your business by thinking like a business owner, getting advice from professionals, evaluating your operation on a regular basis. Doing that will go along way in helping you become a success rather than a statistic.

It always amazes me how many people get into the trucking industry as Owner Operators without doing the proper research for the business. If they had they would have completed a business plan to show exactly how they will be getting paid, what their goals are for the business, and how they plan to get there. The business plan is also the key in getting funding for the business through banks and finance companies. So why do people go though that investigative phase without doing the homework?

Many start looking at becoming an Owner Operator as a way of securing a job. if you buy a truck it will get you on with a certain type of company and so they begin the journey. When the company doesn't work out however they are now locked into a contract with payments, maintenance issues and so on. Once you have made the decision to become an Owner Operator you are essentially locked in for at least four years. Making that type of commitment deserves proper investigation and that should be done in the form of a business plan. What is your action plan for survival? What will help you make a profit when your workload is up and down due to hours of service issues, weather, etc. How many miles a week will you need to break even and meet your monthly commitments. These issue can't be taken lightly and need to be thoroughly investigated.

Any driver needs a road map to help them take the most efficient route to their destination, as a professional driver you would evaluate that route for low bridges, scale crossings, residential areas, mountain driving, and other obstacles. You would try to stay on the interstate for as long as you can and make the most of highway driving. Getting to your destination in a timely fashion and being on time are paramount to getting reloaded and making money in the transportation industry.

So why wouldn't you do the same thing when going into business for yourself? You want the same things. You need a road map to help you get to your destination, you want to evaluate your route for obstacles, and you want to reach your destination in a timely fashion. You wouldn't drive blindly around the country hoping to end at your destination, so don't drive your business blindly down the road, create that map, the business plan!

Some feel they have that because they have done that in the past but then never revise it or even look at it again. The new people coming out of truck driving school have a habit of looking at this industry to death, but all in the wrong places because they don't develop their plan on paper. If you are going to do all kinds of homework, go to seminars, talk with recruiters and different companies, don't you think taking a note pad around and a pen would be a good idea. It amazes me to see the people that pick a career this way or decide to get into business without writing it all down on paper. Just listening you will not remember the important details of a presentation.

Without seeing data listed side by side on a piece of paper it is very hard to evaluate an opportunity properly. That is if generally you are looking at the industry, but what if you are starting a business, buying your own truck, then a whole new set of comparisons are required. You need a business plan if you are in start up mode, evaluating your operation, or planning on expansion. Most people don't so this and they miss the boat every time.

These are the ones that complain they are not making any money. They don't have an action plan, they don't have reference as to where they started, are they ready to expand or buy new equipment? As they say the numbers don't lie and can be the best determining factor of what you need to be doing to reach your goals. A proper business plan will encompass a budget, a snap shot of how you will run your business, your goals for the future, and the particulars of how your business is set up. Some information may be straight forward, but having it all in one place will help keep you focused on what needs to be done. Once you have completed your business plan or action plan it is time to start doing the work, follow your plan keeping money aside to fund your business, repairs and so on. Review your plan on a regular basis, I prefer quarterly or semi annually, but I know people who do it monthly or annually, it will depend on the scope of your business but as a business owner it is important to have a handle on your business at all times. Once you have reviewed the business plan you will need to make adjustments as needed. The best way to do that is to sit down with your business consultant or accountant, your profit and loss statement and your action plan and revise what needs to be changed and adjust to coincide with your goals that you set out for your business.

As business owners we all need advice to help us get started and to keep us operating in a successful manner. Whether you are putting together your next business plan or figuring out the best truck to buy as an owner operator you need qualified people to help you. Now there are qualified people all over the world these days and with the internet they seem to come out of the woodwork in droves, however you need to seek out the truth and what is good for your business. The final decision ends with only one person, and that is you. You can say yes or you can say no, but only you can say it. Let me show you how this works.

An Owner Operator bought an older truck from a dealer, frustrated with his fuel mileage he began reading up on how to improve his overall mileage on the road. In one of the many columns that he read it said that if he wanted to improve his mileage he should change his tires to what they call super singles, which are an equivalent to dual tires. Now here is where the personal decision comes in, the owner operator only looked at one part of the equation, not the whole scenario. The advice he had read may have been correct, but the circumstances may have been different. Thinking he was being smart he went to the dealer and asked their thoughts on the project. The dealer told him it wasn't worth doing because his truck was so old the change wouldn't be justified. The owner operator wouldn't listen and went to seek out the advice somewhere else. The truck was only worth around $20,000 and changing the tires would have cost around $7000 and he would not have created enough of a savings in the change to warrant the tire change. The owner operator decided to go ahead with the change, but one thing stopped him. He didn't have the money, he would have had to borrow it from the company and they had already lent him money.

If you are going to seek out advice, keep yourself set in reality. The condition of the truck was not worth the change the owner operator was looking to make. He would have been better set to pay off his debts, operate profitably and trade up to a newer truck that may have had the tire package he was looking for. Sometimes to be successful you need to make sure there isn't something in front of you holding you back. Let's just hope that something isn't you!

Nowadays many companies hire consultants on a regular basis to provide information and opinions on a variety of products and services. In the transportation market alone there are many consultants especially in the field of safety and driver training that are either employed or freelance to many industry clients. Whether you're big or small at some point in your business career you will need the help of a consultant to help keep your business running profitably. So if you do decide you need a consultant what should you look for, what types of things do you need to know.

First take the price equation out of the picture, not that you shouldn't focus on price, but that should not be your initial focus. Price can be evaluated after other areas of expertise have been established. The first areas of expertise is knowledge, does this person focus on a few areas of expertise or a list of 100 topics. Many of us have a few areas of strong topics that we are known for in the industry. Does the consultant work regularly in your industry? I see this many times companies will bring in someone from outside of their industry to give a presentation, sometimes you can get away with that depending on the reason for the session but for important topics try to get someone from the industry you are in so that the audience can relate better to the presenter. Will the presenter relate to your audience? If the person giving a presentation can't relate to the people in the audience your message won't have a hope in getting across.

When looking at the work a consultant make sure you are able to track progress of the work, did they do their job? Are they following the time lines set out during the proposal stage, are they giving regular reports and did they explain everything up front as to what will be done and how it will be done?

Many business owners especially owner operators feel they don't need a consultant to help them, that the cost outweighs the profits. Well, that is the wrong way to think of hiring a consultant and like I said before price is the last evaluation on the list. A consultant for your business may be the best thing you could do to help make your business successful. A consultant will bring a number of things to the table. First they will bring a fresh set of eyes to your business, you may have been too close to the business to see potential problems. Second a good consultant will set you on a track to success by creating an action plan and a review plan to make sure you are staying on track. Next your consultant will be someone of high integrity that you can trust and is dedicated to seeing your business be successful. Think of a consultant as your personal success manager. A good consultant is like a good accountant, if they know their stuff then you will save money instead of spend money. The first step on your end is to make the call and then trust them to be there for you.

First let me suggest that you need a proper accountant if you're going to be in business. You can choose to do the bookkeeping yourself if you choose, but an accountant is critical to the success of your business. Many new business owners tell me that the cost of an accountant is too much to spend when starting out and I can understand that because they don't come cheap. However a good accountant will save you money in the long run therefore paying for themselves over time The important part is to get someone you trust and is knowledgeable of all the tax laws. That being said, even with a good accountant you will either need a bookkeeper or need bookkeeping software to keep your business running. Remember when evaluating the cost of software to include the true cost of the software, your time! That's right the numbers won't jump into the computer system on their own, either you put them there or someone else does.

There are many different types of systems on the market so which one you decide to use is entirely up to you but there are some things you should watch to make sure you have success using the programs.

The first rule I have is make sure the software you are using is what your accountant is using. The main software I see in offices is Quickbooks and it is very good. The point is that you want software that can be updated and clarified by your accountant and then imported back into your own system. This way you will be using proper numbers when evaluating your profit and loss statements. Find software that works with your business, as an owner operator most standard software will work, but if you have another type of business that requires estimates, statements, payroll or any of the other functions then make sure the version or software you buy has those functions or else it useless to you. Ensure the software is user friendly and something you can grasp quickly or it may cost you more in time to learn it or be a waste of money all together.

Once you have decided on a program take it to your accountant and get them to set up your chart of accounts for you, it is extremely important that you do that from someone who knows the tax tables and categories. This will make it easier for your bookkeeping duties and easier for the accountant at year end. Really evaluate the costs of doing this yourself. Delegating this task to someone who knows what they're doing will save you money in the long run and free up time for other important duties. Remember your time is worth something so include it in all evaluations.

Should You Incorporate Your Business or Not?

As I speak with many new drivers and owner operators I get asked the question quite often to whether they should incorporate their business or not. There are some very important things to think about when deciding on moving forward with incorporation, however most owner operators don't look at the total picture. Much focus on the cost and the cost can vary because it is based upon the assets you have for your business and the type of business you are in, but these costs are small when you look at the big picture over time. The costs are also a lot less in the beginning as opposed to later in your business when you have more assets to worry about. Your costs also will go up for bookkeeping and accounting fees, but again that will help in the long run to keep your company viable. Even as a sole proprietor you will have those expenses just on a smaller scale. So let's look at the benefits of incorporation and why it is a smarter choice for the long term.

In my mind anyone who is planning on making $80,000 or more per year in their business should look at incorporation, maybe not the first year but eventually because it will help tax wise and show that you are in the business for the long term. Many people view sole proprietors as people not very serious about their business. If your business has opportunities for you to be sued or have other liabilities then incorporation is important because it helps to protect your personal assets. Some larger corporations will not work with businesses that are not incorporated so incorporation helps you with contracts and other business options. If you are looking for funding options many banks and financial institutions require that you be incorporated. Tax breaks are one of the most important advantages to being incorporated as corporations are taxed at a lower rate than other types of business models.

That advantage alone is enough to offset the cost of incorporating. If you ever wanted to sell your business or parts of your business you need to be incorporated to sell a business. The other major advantage is that as a corporation you become an employee and are able to regulate your salary to be the best tax situation for you personally. This helps you pay a much smaller tax rate helping you save much needed cash flow. So how do you set yourself up to be incorporated?

There are a number of ways to do this. If you are just starting out in your business then you can complete the filing application online. You can also visit your local small business development centre and complete this at their office. If you have many assets to include in your business or if you feel that the process may be too involved then I would suggest working with a lawyer that works with business law. In all cases I would suggest getting advice from people that understand the incorporation process. Incorporating online can range anywhere from $250 to $1000 and lawyers would of course have additional fees. Remember that you are going into business for the long term and part of your success comes from starting your business out on the right footing. Structure builds houses, roads, and businesses. If you don't have a plan then you will have a hard time knowing if you have reached success in your business.

Okay you have decided to go into business for yourself and wonder what you will need to keep the engine running smoothly. As someone who works with many new Owner Operators some are petrified and have done nothing in the way of preparing for the operation side of their business, where others have gone overboard and created logos and other things that won't be needed. The ideas of business is usually flamed by dreams of rich success, truck loads of money, and days to squander how you wish. Although that can happen the reality is usually far from that and can burst a hole in your bubble large enough to fall through. We all want a corner office with a view, and assistant to schedule our time, and lunches with rich clients. If you were becoming the President of Apple Computers that may be your expectation. So as an Owner Operator what do you need to get things going towards a smooth operation?

I am going to assume here that the truck side has been worked out. In other words you will have a truck and will be the primary driver. Many people will think that having the truck is the office and that may be true to a point but that shouldn't be your main office, that is the office that will bring in the income. You will need some sort of stable mailing address which for most is their home as an office address. Now don't think at this point you should go rent office space in the local industrial section of town although that may be required if you are going to be a total Independent Carrier with other trucks, but that isn't what I am talking about here. I am talking to the leased on Owner Operator and your home will be fine. If you have an extra bedroom not being used or a corner of the basement, even a closet can all work as an office. You won't need much room, but if possible find a room with a door on it that can be considered a separate office. There are many tax reasons for doing this based on your business setup such as office deductions, utility deductions, and more. These are best discussed with your accountant based on each person's personal situation. In that room you will need a few items that are fairly basic. I will leave furniture up to you but a basic desk and filing cabinet is a good idea. You will need a place to file bookkeeping, invoices, and other paperwork as required.

If you have ever been through any kind of Government audit you will know that record keeping is paramount and as important as greasing the truck. As for computers a printer will probably be needed and I suggest a laptop that you can take with you and work from home with as well. This way during down times you can also handle some work on the road. Unless you have a traditional bookkeeper you will need some accounting software, internet and email account.

Each operation may require different things so tune the information here to what you need for your business and personal life. You don't need to build a new office for someone that will be gone most of the time, but you do need a safe place to store your records. You can always expand as needed so buy and set up just what you need, keeping expenses low is the key to a successful operation. With technology you can do a lot so do your homework first.

One of the hardest areas to work in transportation is as a team unit. You have to spend almost 100% of the time with the other person in a confined space. There have been many stories of people being left by the side of the highway because they couldn't get along. This doesn't account for the trust factor of being able to sleep while another person has control of a rig weighing 80,000 pounds traveling at 100 kilometres an hour.

On paper everything seems to work out like a dream, you and your buddy are great friends, you both can drive, and are both looking forward to seeing the country while making some money. As much as that seems to cover all the bases you may find it not that rosy a picture once you get in the cab. On paper you worry about the big stuff, how will each of you get paid, who will have certain duties and so forth. In the cab the little things are what seem to take over such as your potato chip bag is on my side of the bed, and you take up too much room with your clothes and books. If you're stuck out of town waiting for a load can you stand your partner in cramped corners for two days while you are both tired and looking for a place to rest your head? So how do you do this without killing each other on the way back from a trip or making a person walk the rest of the way home?

Planning is the answer to that question. You really have to know the person that you will be living with for seven days a week. Everyone has their quirks and they don't come out until some time has gone by and it is too late to turn back. To be successful here are some tips to make sure you have covered not only the major points but the small points of successful team driving.

First make sure you know the person extremely well and I am talking about their personal habits here, not just that Bill is a great guy to drink beer with. Have a contract that clearly states who is in charge, what duties each will cover and have an out clause in case things go bad. Divide duties and space fairly, keep clutter to a minimum as with two people in the small confines of a truck can make the space seem much smaller. Have a place that is only for you that is not available to anyone but yourself such as a duffel bag or cabinet. If you buy items such as groceries either shop together, split the bill, or give each person their own shelf in the fridge for their items. Probably the most important is to know when the other person likes to be quiet or needs space to cool down, everyone has their time make sure you know when that is. Many team operations are successful and some are just not worth the time, but the more you know about your partner usually the more successful the operation can become, remember it is just like a marriage, give and take!

Step 6

Buying a Truck

*T*he smell of the diesel, the polished chrome, the freedom of the road, these are all things that draw people to the transportation industry as professional drivers. I can't tell you the feeling you get as you run along the open highway with a nice clean truck, kids are motioning you to honk the horn, and at rest stops tourists are asking to take pictures with your truck. It almost makes you feel like a rock star; however there is more to trucking than looking good and that means making a living. One of the best opportunities in the industry is to become an independent contractor or as they are known an owner-operator. In essence you are a business owner, proud and true. Many owner operators lose that pride factor due to the stress of running a business. it is not uncommon for that to happen and doesn't need to happen if you start things out on the right foot. That means working with quality people and choosing equipment that will help you be successful. We all would like more than we can afford, but in business patience can be your biggest friend. Take your time to lay the foundation for your business before expanding too fast. If you are starting out as an owner operator your first truck should be a responsible, reasonably priced used truck. You will eventually get to those new trucks, but learn your way first. It could be the best first step you make as a business owner.

As a business owner making a truck purchase it is important that you are getting all of the information up front and from a reliable source. Test the people a little bit, make sure they answer all of your questions, find out how long they have been in business, and what is their background. If you work with them you will be making a valuable investment so you want to be comfortable with the process. Don't commit to anything on the first visit and take note how long it takes for someone to speak with you and so on. I always say it is the little things that define a dealer. Do your homework and you will find that being cheated doesn't even come into play.

You may think that it is best to just show up at the dealership with the manufacturer of truck you want and make a deal, but you would be mistaken to go in and complete that deal blindly.
This happened early on to me when I was buying my first car from a dealership. I found the car I wanted and started working with the salesperson without doing my homework properly. After negotiating the details we completed the transaction and I picked up the car. The salesman was not there the day I picked up the vehicle and needless to say some of the items that were discussed were not carried out on their part. They were little things, but even though the unit was used it was new to me and I wanted everything down to the new car smell if possible. I was young and naive in those days and didn't pursue the matters to the best of my abilities. That lesson always left a bad taste in my mouth and to this day I will not deal with that dealership and that was over 20 years ago. The moral of the story is to not rush in without knowing who you are dealing with.

When buying a truck it is more important to know the people you are dealing with rather than the type of truck that buy, why? Because many of the trucks have the same components and can be ordered with the type of truck you want. In the old days if you bought a certain model truck it came with a certain type of engine, etc. Nowadays you can buy the truck manufacturer of your choice, order the engine type you wish, and spec the truck the way you like. So if that is the norm then the important part of the equation is dealing with a reputable dealership and as I explained earlier be able to trust the word of the person to carry out items negotiated during the purchase.

The next piece of the puzzle is to make sure the dealership you work with has the flexibility, network, and support to get you the financing you need in order to be successful. Some dealerships deal with a bank and others have their own financing networks. This is a critical issue especially for new drivers becoming owner operators.

To begin your search gather information on several dealerships in your area, make a day to drive around and get a feel for their inventory, network, and personnel. Narrow your search down to three and then finally down to one that you feel very comfortable dealing with and are sure can deliver the specifications that you require. You may have to settle on some items, but don't settle on items you require for employment or are important to your comfort as a driver. By doing things this way you will feel comfortable with your purchase, will feel good recommending a person to that dealer, and will create a lifelong relationship that can last your owner operator career.

How do you know when it is the right time to look at getting into business for yourself and owning a truck? With the economy just starting to recover and everyone hanging tightly onto their wallets it can be very scary as to whether it is the right time to start a business. The economy flushed a lot of companies out that weren't operating properly and that was needed in many industries and as much as people hate to believe it may even of helped many industries. This is a cleansing process that has to happen from time to time to keep the world revolving in a natural state. In speaking with many truck drivers many would tell you not to get into business now, but I beg to differ. In the business world a downturn like we just went through can be very beneficial and even create opportunities that weren't available before. If you are the type of person that looks at the glass half empty then you may feel like the best idea is to stay away from the business all together. If you are an optimistic person then you will see this as a time of opportunity. In my mind the latter of you are correct. This is a great time for opportunity and getting into the transportation industry. Why is that you ask?

For those of you familiar with the industry you will know that we are going into a driver shortage that is even going to get worse in the near future. There is also a lot of equipment available from other companies and owner operators at great deals that can benefit someone new coming into the market. The third item is that people hopefully have woken up a bit as to operating a little smarter since the economy blew out and systems have been put in place in many companies to help owner operators and the transportation industry as a whole remain successful. The fourth area is people in general want control of their lives and having your own business even though it is hard is one of the ways of doing that. So how do you decide if you are ready for the world of transportation? The only person that can answer that question is you. Evaluate where you are in life and if this will be a step up or a step back. If you're already in transportation you probably know the industry and how it works so you will be ahead of the game. Are you where you want to be in your career, do you want to be in business for yourself, do you have the determination to succeed? These questions only you can answer. If you're not in the industry as of yet and are looking at the opportunities from outside then you have a little more homework ahead of you. Investigate the industry; see if the lifestyle fits with what you want as far as family time, and so on. Plan on a date that you would want to have as a start up date, which will probably be about 12 weeks out or more if you don't yet have the license required and do your homework. Homework is the key to a successful career and business in the transportation industry and good planning can get you there.

Choosing the right truck comes down to more than deciding on a colour, how many stacks it has, and so on, You have to know the type of work you will be doing with it, component size, and more. As mentioned in earlier posts homework is the best line of defense to make sure you get the truck that is appropriate for you. If you're thinking of buying a truck it is important for you understand the company you may lease on with. If the company hauls flatbed and you buy a truck thinking it will handle the load only to find out that a year down the road they want you to pull a set of trains then you may be in for a hard lesson. That truck you bought may not have the drive train and power to get the job done. So when searching out companies make sure to investigate the total scope of their operation, you need to take into account changes within the next three years of your career so you can buy the proper equipment, changing trucks after a year can be mighty expensive and a real problem depending on the financial situation that you are in at the time. If you buy a truck that is not set up properly and change to gravel or an operation where you need wet lines and other add ons your truck may not be set up properly and that can get expensive as well. Never buy a truck based upon what looks good in the dealer's yard, buy a truck based on the equipment you will need for the near future. Your bank account and career will be better off for it!

As usual when buying a truck you are not just buying a truck, you're buying into a business. This has been discussed in prior examples so I won't go into it again here. There is however some things that you must look out for and investigate in order to get a truck that will do the job for you and help make you money. As I always say the best place to start is by doing your homework and that can be started right at your kitchen table. I am going to assume that you have some type of focus as to the type of companies you may be leasing on with. If not then that is your first point to start with. If you've done that homework already then the next step is to get focused on the equipment you will need to get the job done. No you don't need a great big long tractor to do city work; you'll only look cool going in a straight line and it will make the general motorists mad at you for getting stuck in the intersection on a turn. So decide on the type of equipment needed, do you need a truck with wet lines, a straight truck, will you haul oversized loads etc? Then start to break it down into your top three picks.

Take out a piece of paper and create three columns, one with the truck make you prefer, the requirements needed for employment, and your price objectives. Now spend a few days visiting dealerships that deal with that type of equipment and collect material on the trucks available in your price range. You should come home with a wealth of information, and don't forget to evaluate the staff as to how you were treated, their knowledge, and so forth. Now compare the material completely to see the best deal for you. Make sure when comparing trucks you are comparing apples to apples. The components to watch for the most are engine power, transmission, wheelbase, suspension, axle spacing, 5th wheel, and so on. Note that the coolest C.B. Radio or stereo is not on the list. You did get the warranty information didn't you? Compare that as well as that can be a major factor with a used truck. As much as I like chrome forget that for now, it doesn't improve the performance of the truck or help you make more money. Those are the nice to haves that come later in your career. Whatever you do make sure the dealership or seller is reputable. Be very weary of those selling their trucks through a private sale. Remember a truck driver will put on about a 120,000 miles a year and your first truck should last at least three years before considering a trade. In my book, if you deal with good honest people, you will get a good honest truck.

Did you hear the story about Fred who went to work for a new company and was told to drive the old truck they had parked out back? As he refused to drive the old beast he said, "I'll become an Owner Operator and drive what I want." So off he went on the weekend to scope out a brand new piece of equipment, shiny rims, large stacks, the works. Being sold the truck of his dreams many people were happy that weekend and it showed. The salesman who said, "yes that is the one you need" and made a hefty purchase at the jewelery store on the way home, to the kids jumping up and down as Fred pulled in the driveway to wipe off the bug that hit the windshield on the way home. Even Fred's wife thought that the giant truck looked kind of cool. Fred sure felt good driving in the yard on Monday showing off the gleaming piece of machinery he now owned. He was like a celebrity, showing the other drivers his new machine, flashing the lights and honking the horn to impress people passing by. In fact that went on for days until he finally was dispatched with a load. Fred was in his glory.

What Fred didn't realize until months down the road was that life in the transportation industry can be up and down and stuff happens on the road all the time. Delays here, traffic jams there, all eat away at precious miles and time. Eventually the bills became overwhelming and he lost his pride and joy. Fred was disheartened and disappointed. He had learned some hard lessons over the year. He learned he should have spent more time investigating the financial end of purchasing a truck. He also should have looked into who he was dealing with when buying the truck to make sure he was getting sound advice. Those actions alone would have helped Fred be successful. In the end Fred had gone full circle and now was back standing in front of that same old truck parked out back. This is the wrong way to buy a truck. Warranties are another area that you really need to do your homework.

When you start looking to purchase your first truck and evaluating the different warranties on the market you may find it hard to evaluate which one is best for you. This is especially true if you don't know how many miles you will run in any given time. My advice is get as much as you can. First you have to figure out roughly how many miles you will run in a given year. For long haul drivers you are looking at around 10,000 miles a month or even more. Multiply that by 12 and 120,000 miles will be the average. With that in mind a 50,000 mile warranty isn't going to take you very far. Realize that your first truck needs to last at least three years before it is time to trade it in so you want your warranty to go as far as possible.

Once you've evaluated the miles you need to look at the components covered in the warranty. Remember if a motor blows on a truck you could be in for a repair bill that exceeds $15,000 so coverage is essential. You want to make sure all of the major components are covered within the next three years. Go over warranties with a fine tooth comb to make sure you are clear on what is covered. Ask lots of questions and make sure you are comfortable with the answers.
After components look into other programs such as towing, off-site repairs and what possibilities are available in those areas . Tractor trailers require special tow trucks and costs are a lot higher than with a car. Towing coverage may be very beneficial if things break down on the road. Other areas to review are service calls, labour charges and so on. So how do you track all of this so when buying a truck you ask the right questions? The best way is to create a list of possible items to cover when you begin looking for a truck. Another idea is to take a tape recorder with you so you can go over the answers later and take notes. Be sure to let the sales person know you are recording the conversation.

As a consultant one of the most frequently asked questions I get from potential Owner Operators is how much capital do I need to finance my truck? This is a loaded question at best and the answer may be different for everyone. I don't want to scare anyone off but most people don't have the capital required to properly enter the industry as a business owner. Many times the candidate is coming from an unemployment situation and is trying to find a position as quick as possible. Business never operates and delivers a return as quick as we want it so it is not a quick fix situation. In fact it may cost you more to start up than if you just got a job, what if you don't like the industry, you are now stuck with contracts and other items of business that you don't want, but still have to pay so getting into business in a hurry to provide some income will be a disappointment in most cases. So what will you need to get started.

The first piece of the puzzle is the truck, as an Owner Operator you will be expected to provide the tractor unit. Now most new people have been to the truck show and want the fanciest truck they can find, in fact one candidate thought that being an Owner Operator was all about driving a fancy truck around and being paid for it, wrong! You will want a decent used truck to start your business off with. We all want a new truck but that is about three trade ins down the road. Keep your fixed costs low with a good used truck. A used truck within five years of age should cost you around $45-$50,000 giving you a truck payment of around $1500.00 per month. You will need a down payment of around 20% or around $10,000. Now this is the scary part, you can ask family and friends for help, or maybe you have funds somewhere else you can use. A creative way of going about this is asking the carrier or dealership if they offer any incentives to buying from a particular place, many times there are bonuses that can be used toward the down payment to help with the purchase. So lets assume you've scraped up enough money for the truck, but what about the operating costs.

This is where business becomes really fun. Not too often the company will pay right out of the gate, you need to run some miles first. You can also expect to be about 15 days late with each trip before you get paid. That first month will be the hardest as everything is starting at once, but you will need at least enough operating capital for one months operating costs with the exception of fuel. The company will most likely have a fuel program that will be billed directly to your statement, even though it's been done before resist the use of using traditional credit cards to operate your business, that can get out of hand in a hurry. Some costs may come off your statement but you need to account for them. First your personal costs, you need to eat and pay the mortgage, support your family and so on, so figure out those costs, then add business costs such as phone charges, insurance and so on. Add those costs together and you will come to you monthly amount that you will roughly need to get going.

So if you need $10,000 for your down payment, and another $5000 for your first month you will need $15,000 to get started minus any help you get from dealerships or employers. Partner this with a good budget and you should be on your way to a successful business career.

There are a number of ways to get a truck and much of it will depend on your personal credit rating, your capital for a down payment, the carrier you are signing on with, and the number of years in the industry. Add to that the various options of traditional leasing, options for buying a truck, and of course the in-house lease plans through carriers.

Leasing and buying a truck each have their own advantages and disadvantages depending on your own situation and capital attained. So this will be the first step in determining the direction you need to go. Financing options will be determined by your credit history and how well you have managed that side of your life. So lets look at buying or leasing by themselves. When you buy or lease truck you are creating a fixed expense for your business. Whatever number you negotiate will be there for the next five years or length of contract you were able to sign on with. The goal of the business owner is to keep fixed costs as low as possible. If you're buying the truck going in with a higher down payment will give you the best deal for a lower payment. Buying a good used truck over the bright shiny new truck will give you a lower payment. Now remember the goal is to keep your fixed expense as low as possible so negotiating a deal with no down payment will give you a larger fixed payment on a monthly basis. If you buy a truck you can modify it within reason as you like within the warranty. You want that big Texas bumper go ahead and put it on, so you gain some flexibility there. You are also building equity in the payments leaving you with ownership of the truck in the end, and you gain the options such as writing off the depreciation and taxes if the truck is purchased.

If you're leasing your truck your payment pay be lower or higher than buying depending on your credit rating. People many times go the leasing route as the down payment is usually considerably lower which is the appeal but you have to be aware of some of the pitfalls of leasing. When leasing you don't own the vehicle at the end, it is much like a rental agreement. You make your payments and after the term of the lease is expired you have the option of returning the truck to the dealership or buying the truck out at the end. This may seem like the smart way to go but depending on how well the truck was cared for on the road it can be costly. Depending on your business setup you may be able to write off the payments for the lease, but it may cost you more in taxes at the end if you decide to purchase the unit. If you buy the unit and turn it over afterward then you may pay more than the unit is worth. With a lease changing or modifying the truck may be out of the question. Any customization would change the lease agreement because the truck should be turned back in in the same shape other than normal wear and tear as when you picked it up. If either of these options don't work there is one other option known as an in-house lease.

An in house lease is when a carrier has their own equipment and leases it much in the same as traditional lease but with more restrictions. For instance many times you never get to a point where you own the vehicle as the trucks are turned over in certain time periods. You can't move the truck to another carrier if you find the one you are with not working out. Many drivers end up leaving and have in essence paid for a truck driving job. All the control of the lease is in the carriers hands with very little flexibility for the owner. The reason these are popular is you usually get new equipment with essentially nothing down. Some are good but many are not worth while for the long run. If you have the money for a regular down payment then go a traditional route where you buy or lease the truck yourself and sign it on with a carrier. If you do go this route do your homework and read the agreement very carefully.

If there is one true thing about anything mechanical is that it will eventually break down no matter how well it was built. That my friends is just a fact of life and something that needs to be taken into account. Upgrading equipment however is not an easy task for most due to the capital investment required, operational restrictions, and financing options. So how do you plan for equipment while making sure you haven't bit off more than you can chew?

First drawing up that plan from the start is key and should be worked into your business plan from the start. You will have to replace equipment down the road and you may as well start looking at that now. Your maintenance budget should be included as a key factor to helping you determine when you should start looking at replacing equipment. You also should be in touch with your accountant as to how your depreciation is affecting your taxes and ideal times to be trading or replacing equipment. Your budget for the truck will be your payment plus down payment, plus maintenance budget. If you have a newer truck then you may have a lower maintenance budget, but if your truck is older you should have a higher maintenance budget to compensate for that. Hopefully your truck isn't breaking down regularly so your maintenance money should be building up into a bit of an equity float for you. If your truck has been breaking down a lot then your funds are probably low in the maintenance area. There is one more thing to factor in to your decision and that is the amount of down time that the truck has cost you due to break downs. On average a break down of two to three hours can cost you approximately 400 miles. At a dollar per mile plus the expense you have lost that is big money to your business. As I said before all things mechanical will break down, how you manage those break downs are the key to success. If you are reviewing your profit and loss reports on a regular basis you will find out the critical information you need to assess your own situation about replacing your truck. Going the extra mile of taking things like oil analysis, fuel samples, and more will help you determine what your truck is doing on the inside and if you should start looking at replacing your equipment sooner than later. This will put you a step ahead in knowing the right time to replace your equipment.

Where do you replace that equipment and when you are ready to make that step? If you are looking for new equipment then any of the big truck manufacturers have retail showrooms around the country. If you are looking for older equipment then start with a reliable truck reseller, if you can't find what you're looking for there then other options include truck auctions, private sales, and so on. Be very careful with private sales as a good deal may not be such a good deal down the road. Make sure to check things like warranties, maintenance histories and so on. The important thing is to have a plan so that you are replacing your equipment before it is replacing you.

If you're like me you will be asking yourself if I am crazy to suggest you go to an auction to upgrade your equipment. The answer is no or yes depending on how you look at it. Much of that will depend on where you are in your career or what you are trying to do with your business. Auctions are not for the faint of heart, you need to know what you're doing, what to look out for, and do your homework on the vehicles available. Don't go to an auction with a cold as you may come out buying 10 trucks at the end, it goes so fast it will blow you away, but the experienced can get themselves some good deals. So how would go about upgrading through the auction? If you are like me you assume an auction house is a place where equipment goes that is no longer needed and isn't fit for the road. If you have ever seen some of the famous car auctions on television you will notice the opposite, that these auctions are where you go to find rare models and get good deals.

On television the auctions are high priced vehicles, but of course we are on the other end of the spectrum. The truth about auctions for the most part is that it is a place for dealers to keep moving their equipment to make space in the yards for newer inventory and that is where the deal comes in for you.

One thing about buying from the auction is to have money set aside to invest in your purchase. Most equipment will need some type of work invested in it to bring it up to par. That can range anywhere from a good cleaning to an engine rebuild. Think of it this way, if you buy a truck for $10-20,000 at the auction in decent condition, invest another $10,000 into it afterward you would have a truck that could take you another two or three years with little payments. This is a great way to add a second truck onto your business or expand your small fleet.

Here are some tips when going to the auction to help you come out successful. First know what you're looking for ahead of time as not every auction date will have the equipment you need. Payments and deposits happens right after the transaction so have the appropriate funds ready to go. Take someone with you that is knowledgeable with equipment and get to the auction early to look over the equipment before the bidding starts. Go to an auction first just to get the lay of the land as the pace can be very intimidating. The auction isn't for the faint of heart but with some homework it can be a great place to get a great deal.

Running by the Mile - 10 Steps to a Successful Trucking Business

Step 7

Operating your Trucking Business

ob had been a great driver his whole career. He had worked his way up from bad companies to good companies, and now had solid credentials as a professional driver. He had great time management, knew his way around the country, kept his truck like his own, and wasn't afraid to take a trip to an area he wasn't familiar with. Bob had been driving for about 15 years and was getting the itch to move on to something new, and thought becoming an Owner Operator may be the best way to satisfy that itch. Bob started his investigation into what was needed to become an Owner Operator by asking everyone at the truck stops what they knew about the business, and at the end the only thing he got was a headache. Everyone told him something different and many of them told him to stay away and forget about the idea. No one told him what is really needed to succeed as a successful business owner. Bob being the smart person that he was decided to go a different route, he hired a professional consultant to help him find the right information.

Once he found a knowledgeable person in the industry they started working together with his goals. Finding that Bob wanted to run under his own authorities down the road they began creating a business plan around that idea. He would start running with a company and down the road if he wanted to he could start adding steps to be a truly independent carrier. Since the company he was with was willing to take him on as an Owner Operator he was able to attain the payment package allowing them to make a detailed budget of items Bob will need when starting his business. With working capital he had saved up he had enough to buy a good used truck and get him started down the road for a few months. With the plan laid out so he knew how much he was paying himself and how much he had to set aside for things like maintenance Bob was able to make decent decisions as to which runs he should focus on and how many miles he needed to run to make sure his business was profitable. He knew how long he would need to work each month to break even and the best way to shop for fuel and other services. After finding a decent accountant and bookkeeping service he found he was able to focus on the driving part of his job allowing him to be a safe operator. The biggest change however was his mindset. After working with his consultant he found the business mindset that is so important to becoming a successful Owner Operator. Bob has done the groundwork to becoming a successful business owner in the transportation industry. The rest was a matter of practicing what he learned.

Once you begin the trip as an Owner Operator it can be a very daunting process trying to keep track of all the different parts of the business. There is the business and maintenance side, and the driver side and they all demand your attention. If you are running your first trip or in the beginning stages of your career then you may feel overwhelmed by it all. The best way to beat that feeling is to break down your time and manage it in small pieces. How do you do that and still make it through without wanting to throw it up to the wind?

As mentioned you have three areas of owning your truck and they are all crucial to your survival. So lets' focus on the next 60 days of being the boss of your new trucking company. If you have just bought the truck I hope you were smart enough to buy or have some kind of warranty for your truck in the case of a breakdown. So on the maintenance side you really only have to worry about changing the oil on a regular basis for the next two months.

Ask your company who they use for maintenance or find someone on your own that you trust to do a good job. Other than small adjustments you shouldn't have a whole lot of maintenance in the first couple of months if the truck you bought was in decent shape.

On the business side you should be trying to arrange for your bookkeeping, taxes, and setting up your budget so you have a good idea on the type of money you need to set aside in each category. A good business consultant can help you set that up and using a program that handles everything for you is the best way to get your business started on the right foot. Once you have set up your system it is just a matter of keeping your receipts and mailing them into the bookkeeper on a monthly basis. Make sure you keep a record of your trips either through invoicing or a journal or you may find you are losing more money than you know.

Now the important part, the driving and operation of the truck. With the other two areas taken care of this will need your undivided attention. This is all practical so keep focused on getting better through improving your time management, understanding border crossings, and all the other duties that go with driving a truck. Focus on getting along with dispatch and ask questions if you are not sure what to do, don't be shy and not ask to find out it cost you big money for something that could have been handled easily right up front.

By focusing on little parts of those areas you will build your business in small steps and not get so overwhelmed with the whole process.

Ah the budget process, nobody likes it, we all shy away from it, yet it returns to haunt us every time. People shy away from it because it shows them where they really are with their business and their life. It can be a very daunting piece of the puzzle but is one of the most important items you can complete when becoming an owner operator. If you try to get away without completing the budget process you will find that you will be at a loss as to where your money has gone. I believe that is why many people don't do the budget because they feel they will have to stick with it or they will be a failure. The fact is that you risk failure without it. By missing this important item you will have nothing to compare your profit and loss statement to know how you are doing in your business. I recently met with some owner operators that were just starting out. They felt the best way to approach compensation with their truck was to take half the money for themselves and leave the rest for their truck. When we completed the budget they could see that they were quickly taking themselves deep into the barrel of despair.

If you are an Owner Operator it is your duty to run your truck as a business owner, it is your job to make sure your company is running successfully. A budget will be one of the first things you do to make sure you can afford to run your business. You should then match that budget with your profit and loss statement on a quarterly basis and again at the end of the year. Review items that seem to be out of control and look for other options that may help bring your budget back in line. Remember that this process is ongoing and not something that should be done just once and then stopped. The true successful business owner is watching their business for opportunities and ways to improve their success rate.

I was at an event that was featuring Dragon's Den star Kevin O'Leary. The event was an investment night put on by a local mutual fund company that carries O'Leary Funds which is Kevin's fund. For those that have never watched the fame show Dragon's Den or the US version named Shark Tank the shows feature potential entrepreneurs pitching their products or ideas to the Dragon panel (there are 5 panel members) hoping to get much needed funding and business help to take their businesses to the next level. Some are shot down and others are granted their wish and have someone from the panel invest in their business. Just being on the show usually catapults a business into success as even the unsuccessful pitchers usually gain ground just by being on the show. If you have ever watched the show you will know that Kevin is known as "Mr Wonderful" by himself and as the hard nosed investor on the show. The event started out with stories from the television shows and basic background about how Kevin became the entrepreneur that he is today. As the evening progressed he kept focusing on one thing for the most part, cash flow! He talked a lot about funds and dividends and such but for the most part the focus was on being flexible by having good cash flow management.

As business owners we know that cash flow is very important, but also realize that most operations run on debt and credit. Many times in business suppliers pay in a certain time period, or income slows down or something happens in life that is unexpected and creates havoc in the business. Having a healthy cash flow in your business can mean the difference between life and death. That however is easier said than done and it takes some serious will power to get going in the right direction.

If you're looking for ways to increase your cash flow it starts with looking at the books for your business and finding out where our cash is going. You may have to keep track of your spending for a while if you haven't done so up to now. Look at your income and look for patterns when money is coming in and when it is due to go out. Creating a schedule for paying bills can help and doing things like allocating a certain amount per mile to go to cash flow are a couple of options for you. Try to pay your bills after you are paid so you are not relying on credit. Try to use cash, but keep track and leave your debit cards and credit cards in your wallet. Cash flow is not rocket science but it seems to baffle most people. Many times it is just a matter of watching more closely the flow of your operation, as Kevin says, "Cash is King!"

It totally amazes me how many Owner Operators get their income statements from the company and either believe it is true without challenging it or even worse don't review it to make sure it is correct. This happens too often and the reason is because many Owner Operators don't understand the deductions that are taken off or didn't realize they were paying for such items. I have talked previously about creating your own invoicing system, every company has one and the Owner Operator should be no different. The important thing is that you understand the statement you receive from the company and you match it to loads you have already pulled and track any expenses that need to be deducted as expenses.

If you accept the statement as gospel then that is the same as accepting a payment from a client and never reviewing it against the invoice. It could be short paid, not paid the tax, etc. As a business owner it is up to you to make sure you receive the money that you have earned to keep your company solvent. If not, the road to bankruptcy is just around the corner. Remember that income is king! Make sure you have all that is coming to you in your business or you will be out of business

When you're a new or potential Owner Operator it can be very confusing as to what type of truck you should buy, how much you should pay for payments, and maintenance, etc. Add in the extra information received about running on a per mile basis and it changes the whole picture as to the type of truck you should buy. So how do you figure this out?

First of all get all of the information you can in regard to a decent truck payment, maintenance costs, and shop time rates and so on. These are important so you know how much you may spend a month on equipment costs as a whole. Then figure out your per mile rate, which you can't do until you do some homework on the type of company you want to lease on with. Let's assume for the sake of argument that the company will pay you $1.00 per mile. I know that is low, but it makes for easy math. So you expect to drive 10,000 miles per month giving you a monthly income of $10,000. Maintenance costs should be budgeted about $1000 per month, and your truck payment on a quality used truck should be around $1500 per month. Now once you start to run you want to keep your maintenance costs and truck payment separate. When trying to figure out cost comparisons such as this then you can group them together. So you have $1000 for maintenance and $1500 for your truck payment. Together you have $2500 per month divided by 10,000 miles which gives you 25 cents per mile as your equipment costs.

Now as an Owner Operator you have to decide do I want to take the chance on a higher payment with a newer truck or take the chance of higher maintenance costs on an older truck? Since you're reading the article anyway let me add my two cents, go with the latter option. If you buy a quality used truck you're maintenance costs may remain low giving you more equity in your business, relieving stress because you have a lower truck payment, and keeping your cost per mile under control. If you buy the newer truck you may have the lower maintenance costs, but the higher truck payment will remain a fixed cost per mile that you can't reduce. When you are starting out you want to keep that flexibility as you learn the ropes of the industry. Time flies when you're in business and learning new things and before you know it you will be trading into your next truck. Remember manage your costs and maximize your profits.

$$$

Sample budget on next page

Owner Operator Initial Budget

Monthly Income

Income Type	Amount
Monthly Net Income / 10,000 miles per month @ $1.10 per mile	$11,000
East Coast Surcharge /per mile /.05 per mile	$500
Surcharge @ .30 per mile	$3,000
Monthly Income	$14,500
Amount per mile	$1.45

Additional Income

Details	Month	Amount
Mid Year Bonus		
Year End Bonus		
Total Additional Income		$0

Monthly Personal

Personal Expenses	Costs
Rent /Mortgage	$1,000
Food /Home	$400
Clothing	$100
Utilities	$150
Phone	$100
Car Payment	
Car Fuel /Repairs	$150
Entertainment	$100
Credit Card Payments	$200
Taxes	$0
Other / Child Support	
Personal Expenses	$2,200

Monthly Truck

Truck Expenses	Costs	Per Mile
Truck Payment	$1,500	$0.15
Company Holdback	$300	$0.03
Truck Maintenance	$1,000	$0.10
Truck Insurance	$100	$0.01
Fuel Tax		
Fuel @ $4.00 g/6 miles/ g	$6,667	$0.67
Professional Fees	$200	$0.02
Payroll	$2,200	$0.22
Disability Insurance	$100	$0.01
Telephone Expenses	$100	$0.01
Food Expenses	$200	$0.02
Total Monthly Expenses	$12,367	$1.24

Profit Margin by Month

Profit
$14,500
$12,367
$2,133.00
.21 per mile

Sample Budget for Owner Operators

Total monthly personal will be your salary
in the monthly truck budget. To get your per
mile rate multiply your amount by .0001

There is one item in business that is the key to success, the engine that drives your car, the most important paper in the filing cabinet, the invoice. For most of us in business that is the key to getting paid and to moving your business forward. If you are not creating invoices, then you are not getting paid. This is normal practice for traditional business that trade products and services in the general course of business, but what about the owner operator. He doesn't need an invoice because he receives a statement, wrong! In speaking with owner operators all over the province about their profit and loss statements many of them would benefit from creating an invoice for their work. Most people don't like to do any extra work but by creating an invoice for your work it gives you a clear picture into how much you are really earning. It is an extra step that so many would benefit from by taking the time to do it properly. Here is why I like an invoice.

Statements are issued by your company; they also have a variety of items on them such as fuel payments, plates, hold-backs, and so on. They are also usually a month behind of what you actually have run due to the process of collecting data by the person in charge of payroll. So many owner operators when they get their statements are not getting a true picture of what they are getting paid for and even worse some do not know if they are being paid for all of their miles. The fact that they do not have an invoice tracking their income gives them no recourse should they have to fight the company for funds at a later date. Have you ever heard someone wining that they aren't making enough money and when you ask them to show how they got to that point they have nothing to show you, no evidence to back up their claim other than a broke bank account. Bank accounts mean nothing in the world of business, many successful companies have no money in their accounts, assets, and invoiced sales, among other factors are what drive business. The company isn't giving you a pay check, you are billing them as a customer, and it is up to you to make sure you are being paid for your work, not the company.

So how do you start? First of all you have to make this a habit, do it all the time always. It won't work if you only do it for one week. Second of all start at the beginning of a month. This way you have a nice clean break. Now if you are a driver only each time you get back to you terminal photocopy your trip envelope or print off your run sheet, however your company does their trip reporting. That becomes your invoice so to speak. If you are an owner operator I want you to create an invoice on a weekly basis showing where you went, your trip number, and your income made for that trip. You don't have to send it off to anyone, but when you receive your statement if you are using software or by hand you can check off that you have been paid for the trip. At the end of the year you will know exactly how much income you earned, if you have been paid properly, and how long it took you to be paid. Should you be looking to purchase a truck or trying to get funding you will have proper invoices to show to help you make your case to the financial institution. This is considered due diligence, successful companies do it, so why don't you?

You may find this to be a funny question but it can be dreadfully true in some cases. As a professional driver or Owner Operator our reputation used to be built on helping people stuck at the side of the road, almost like the road warrior theory. It wasn't a thought to help some lady change a flat tire, or use your phone to call for help.

I remember when I was hauling chemicals for a company it was owned by a Canadian outfit and I had stopped one day to help an elderly couple fix a flat tire, taking a total of 10 minutes. I had been in that situation before as have most of us and being stuck at the side of the road is no fun. No one else seem to be stopping, anyhow after I left she wrote a thank you letter and sent it to my company. They were happy at what I had done, that our company culture was that of helping others and so on. A few years later the situation happened again,but when the office found out I was told not to do that again. That I had put the company in danger of being hit, or the truck stolen, etc. Since then we were told not to stop and help people at the side of the road due to liability of insurance. Apparently our company culture had changed.

So the question is what is your company saying on this subject and are you putting your company at risk by helping others. I am sure there is no right or wrong answer for this one but it is food for thought. With theft in transportation rising, traffic getting busier every day stopping on the side of the road is frowned upon by most companies and I can understand those factors. What scares me is my belief system that what goes around comes around, and what you put out you get back! If that's the case then the world will stop helping each other in times that seems like we need people to band together more than ever. I myself will continue to help people stuck at the side of the road if the need arises, to me helping others is what we are all about.

But what about you, what is your policy, what is your company policy? That may be a question for the next safety meeting. Better to know now than later. This may even bring into light another problem, what happens when you or those in your company don't agree with you?

As a business owner there are many tasks that you are responsible for and probably handle yourself. Everything from signing the big deal to cleaning the washroom may be in your list of jobs to be done at any given time. That is the joy and life of most entrepreneurs. Although many of us are good at multitasking we generally know quite a bit about several parts of our business but not everything. That is where the board of advisors come in for your company. The board may differ from company to company but usually consists of your accountant, your financial planner, your banker, and a business consultant. You may have more or less depending on the size of your business. Having all theses people on your board may make you feel that you've got a decent team behind you, that you will get financial and business advice that helps you grow. What happens however when the team doesn't agree? When you are a small business keeping cash flow running smoothly can be a creative task especially if you have debt and obligations to pay. So as you are trying to do your best you are being told different things from each advisor, and the problem is that they are all right.

Here is what happened to us, we were trying to pay down debt and improve our financial picture. My partner and I had made a sound decision not use credit cards if at possible and live on cash. Our financial planner was elated and said that was the way to go. As our accountant was doing our taxes we were going over expenses and he said that it would be better to be paying certain items with the credit card as it helps in tracking items better in the long run, also the right advice.

Our business consultant said try to increase your cash flow by reducing debt meaning that we should pay by cheque whenever possible, also the right advice. By now you are probably starting to see the disconnect that was starting between the advisors.

In the end the final decision comes down to you as as business owner. The team are advisors only and you have to do what is best for your situation. Just like the President you have to weigh each decision against the actual situation. When advisors give you advice they are advising from their outlook on the situation, which will be different for everyone. You have to make the best possible decision for your business based upon the facts and the best case scenario. Welcome to the world of business. These advisors are there for a reason however, if you ever had the tax man call for an audit you will realize how intimidating this experience can be. You will be glad to have that team of advisors at that point.

Considering previous experience I will tell you that you had better have your stuff together if you plan on making it through an audit slightly unscathed. Audits can be very intimidating and scary for most of us. If you think that the big scale guy is intimidating try dealing with the Canada Revenue Agency or the Internal Revenue Service. That is scary on a whole level above the rest. They don't understand things like my computer crashed last month that was holding all the company records, or that you didn't track your mileage to the safety meetings because you forgot. When we went through the audit for our business I was amazed at the information I was asked to provide. They didn't want to know about the big things like the income and expenses from major clients, they wanted to know why the coffee shop meal was being written off. The expenses that most of us overlook as they are only a few dollars were the focus of their investigation. Now that we have successfully made it through the audit process with just a minor adjustment I wonder how many people are not ready for an audit.

Audits do two things for your business, you either begin to run a tighter ship or you decide this isn't for you and close up shop. For those who decided against getting professional help for their business may fall into the latter because the process is very intimidating to people not in that line of work. We did have a computer crash in one of our years that has created a file that holds some serious financial data and it is only by luck that was not the period that the CRA wanted to look at. That audit made us run better which according to my accountant is the educational component that the CRA tries to do with the clients it audits. They may need to work on their delivery skills a little. They say they use it to educate companies on the proper way to account for their business, that may be true but I think there are better ways to do that.

So I ask you again, would your business pass an audit if you were selected for one? Many of us business owners especially the smaller ones don't feel they are on the radar for being audited. That is wrong, ask any small business that was selected for audit recently. The best way to pass the audit is to get your ducks in a row now before you are selected because once selected you won't be able to make things up. Get an accountant make sure your bookkeeping is being done properly. The biggest thing is to think like a business owner and that means getting serious about running your business. If you don't I can tell you that you will be out of business before you know it.

You own your truck and things have been humming along for a little while. You've been getting your maintenance done at a variety of shops across the country as the need arises, but is that the best use of your time and money? Many Owner Operators do not take advantage of some of the tools that are available to them to help their business be even more successful. One of those ways would be to seek out a garage or repair facility to regularly provide maintenance for your truck. There are a couple of reasons or doing this, one is to get workmanship done by the garage, and the other is by giving them your work you are getting a better shop rate. This also helps in the timeliness of repairs and scheduling equipment in for regular maintenance. By going into a contract with a certain shop you may become one of their wholesale clients which would give you a lower shop rate, give you priority when booking equipment for maintenance, and the mechanics will get to know your truck and be more in tuned to make you aware of potential problems. So how do you go about doing that when you are just a one truck owner? One truck or not you are a business owner and have a right to talk with shops to get the best bang for your buck. It may not work all the time but it may save you a lot of money in the long run by taking a shot.

Here is how you go about getting started. If you have a national plan with your lease that may be a good area to start, but don't discount the smaller networks and shops. Start by finding a shop local to your home area as much of your work may be scheduled while you are off. Ask about the training level of the mechanics and how are mechanics scheduled for repairs. Find out the size of the network, the availability of parts, etc. Then ask about the payment plans, do they have different levels for regular clients, etc. Don't sign any contracts for longer than a year until you are sure the shop is keeping their end of the contract and you are happy with the service. Once you have a contract in place be loyal to that shop outside of emergency repairs.

By doing this you can save yourself money, manage your costs better, and create a relationship that will help your truck be in top shape. Business ownership includes finding the best for the bottom line of your company and that involves looking at all costs associated with your truck.

The best way to cut down on shop repairs is to know your equipment and utilize it to the fullest without pushing its limits. Overloading equipment and weakening its support system can cause problems not only on the road, but in pocket book by needing replacements sooner.

Fred switched trailers like he always did on Monday afternoons in the yard. Dispatch gave him a number, he hooked up, and down the road he went to pick up another load. He had never paid attention to trailers before because they were all the same, however this was different, this one was a reefer unit. The company had recently bought a couple units to try and Fred was lucky enough to get one today. When he loaded the load he didn't think about the weight because that was what he always hauled. As he went down the road he reached the first scale on his trip, and was pulled around back. His truck was overweight and he now had a problem. Realizing his mistake he now had to make a phone call to the company.

When picking up different types of equipment make sure you understand the weight difference in the equipment. A reefer trailer is much heavier than a dry van. Even manufacturers can have different weights and how the trailers are made and materials used can be a large problem. I remember running for a company and having single bunk Freightliner and an aluminum dry van. I was able to haul almost 50,000 pounds and still be legal. After that truck I went to a double bunk Peterbilt, and stainless steel dry van and my weight was reduced by over 3000 pounds. Many times a dispatch department doesn't realize that trailers specifications change by manufacturer or trailer type. To many internal operations personnel trailers are just numbers on the wall or board that need to be assigned to someone. To a driver unaware it can be a very costly situation however, and these days that can also result in problems on your license. As the driver your are the end user and the one responsible for the safe operation of the unit. You are only one person however, so how are you supposed to know all the trailers in the fleet?

Depending on your operation there are a couple of ways to deal with the factor of weight and the equipment. Know your tractor weight as they change dramatically based on frame, engine size, bunk size and more. If you have a dedicated trailer then it is easy, just take your truck empty, full of fuel, and have it weighed at a scale. If you don't run a dedicated trailer then you may have to do a little more work. If all the trailers in the fleet are the same size and manufacturer then take one and weigh it with your truck like above. This will give you an idea on the rest of the fleet. If the fleet has many different types of trailers then see if the maintenance or dispatch departments have a weight sheet and calculate your allowable weight for each trailer type. If they don't have this then to be on the safe side I would weigh your truck before you load with each different type of trailer. Get in the habit of weighing your truck after loading to make sure are in compliance with the regulations. It can make or break your pocket book.

In business although watching expenses is very important and must be done creating income is what keeps the engine running in both your business and truck. You are not only representing the company you are leased on with but are also representing your own business. So having good customer service skills are the key to having a successful business and career.

Most drivers and Owner Operators forget the importance of customer service because they don't feel that they have to deal with the clients directly. They are very wrong and in a big way. If you are an owner operator have you thought about who your clients are in reality? Doing this exercise may surprise you if you take it seriously. So let's look at how you affect the clients while conducting deliveries and communicating with clients. If you run the open board you may not concern yourself with customer service because many drivers don't think they will return to that client unless they are on dedicated run. The truth is that any client that ships or receives goods with the company by truck deserves the best customer service available from every driver. In the industry we hear about customer service departments, business executives, and don't see how we are involved in the important aspects of the client but the truth is that each customer has a number of points of contact that the company will be in contact with them. So what are those points?

Usually for any large contracts the top executives or appointed sales force will be involved and that will be the first point and most important in the beginning. That will be the point where all of the negotiations will take place to secure the customer's freight contract.

Once that point is completed it will diminish in contact to a point, but is still a critical point in the process. The next point will be the transport company internal client service department, such as customer service, order management, and so on. This point of contact is also critical and may or may not be in direct contact with the client depending on the order management system. This second point may also be done by a third party such as a load broker or load board service, but is still critical to great client service. The next point is you, the driver and may be the most critical point of all for the company. You are the live person dealing with another live person and basically could be the face of the company. Whether you are dealing with a receiver on the dock, a shipper in the yard, or phoning the front office for directions you are the face of the company and should be representing them as such. How you dress, the way you talk, and the ways you act are all important to how the client views your company. Are you pleasant to be around, are you patient when waiting for the load, is your trailer organized and clean? Or are you the opposite, have a filthy trailer, you haven't showered in a few days, and are tired and grumpy, just a picture of professionalism to be sarcastic. Everyone has a part to play and you need to do yours.

But there is one other customer we haven't discussed and this is the one that can be the most important player of all and also the one that affects your income the most, your company. As an owner operator you are contracted or leased onto your company. That makes your company your main client. That makes dispatch your key contact, and that puts you in a predicament if you can't get along with them. As mentioned earlier every client has at least three points of contact, the executive level, the order management level, and the shipping /receiving level, or in this case dispatch. The reason most drivers and owner operators don't think of their dispatch as clients is because they think like truck drivers. As a business owner you need to think like the president of your corporation. Your company or truck is bidding against many other businesses (your fellow drivers) for the same freight and as usual the best lanes pay the best money. And as we all know even though dispatch is suppose to treat everyone the same and not take sides that doesn't always happen. If they don't like you, you're dead! If they don't like you they give you the load available at the time. If they don't respect you or trust you, they wait to see if you will deliver on time before assigning you a return load. And in some cases if they don't like you they will send you to places that you didn't even know existed and stop you from getting home for a month. So dispatchers are important people to keep happy. They are your primary point of contact for your company and your own business. So how do you offer great customer service?

This will work for any of your customers including the dispatch kind and to sum it up in one word it is SERVICE! Give awesome service to your customers, dispatch, and others and you will be rewarded handsomely. Now I am not going to promise you big money, but my experience in business is it is the little things that make you great. Be on time and reliable; call ahead if delays are possible. Treat everyone with respect and work with them to offer the best service for your clients. Be easy to work with and keep your image clean such as your appearance, and paperwork. Follow up immediately on any issues with a load or client. As I talk about much of the time, take ownership of your position, after all you are the business owner, the customer service agent, and the driver. You are the three points of contact for your company. Act like the professional business that you run!

Two individuals, two different businesses, both are Owner Operators, both with the same company, yet one is losing money and one is doing well. Why is that? I come across this many times as I speak with Owner Operators and other professional drivers in the business. It happens even in the same company, one will do well and the other is struggling to hang on. Some blame the fuel costs, some blame the freight rates and others just blame everybody but themselves. Where I always ask the question is, if that is the case why are so many people in trucking? Most companies are looking for many drivers or Owner Operators yesterday so the freight is there, many of theses companies have been in business for a long time so they have solid bottom lines, and most have fuel programs to help battle the fuel issue. For those of us that have been in other types of businesses where you have to do marketing, proposals, follow ups, and other business activities that may or may not get you the project, as an Owner Operator in business you just have to be available for work. So I don't think it is the industry that's bad.

What I have noticed in speaking with many Owner Operators and colleagues is that it is the mentality of the business owner that makes or breaks the company. That in itself is the reason certain people fail in business. Two people can work for the same company and have totally different experiences. It's like going to the movies, one person may love the film and the other hate it. Does that mean the film is bad? Does that mean the actors failed in their duties of bringing the story of the film to the audience, many times the answer is no! One person enjoys that type of film, or one person was able to relate with a certain character. In business it is the same and that starts with your operation.

Before you go complaining that it is the company that is hurting your bottom line take a good look at your operation. More important than that however, is taking a good look at your mindset. One of the most important areas that people fail is with their mindset. They don't think like a business owner and by thinking that way they don't see some of the obstacles that affect their bottom line. A business owner mindset will always help you to keep refining your business causing it to improve therefore making it successful.

If you feel you are missing the mark in your business, or are wondering why you don't seem to be as successful as others, your mind may be the first place to start. How many times have you heard that truck driver only make around $2.00 per hour when you figure out the wait times, traffic delays and so on.

It amazes me how many people bounce around the country without any kind of plan or thought to how their time is used and how to enhance their career by being more efficient. This is so true for the professional driver. Many go around the country when they're told and feel as though they hold the key in their hands. They arrive when they want, and the famous line heard over many C.B. radios is "I'll get there when I get there!" My question is what time is that? The same driver who exudes his power by saying the phrase mentioned before is also the same one when sitting in the truck stop will belly ache about how many miles they have put in, how they run multiple logbooks, and how when driving they calculate their income and they average $2 per hour driving. The same driver however keeps on going, week after week after week. If you believe you are averaging $2 an hour for your work I want you to take your truck back to your yard, park it, hand in the keys, and quit!

There is a job at McDonald's down the road that will pay you at least ten dollars an hour and your family will thank you for the eight dollar an hour raise that you just got, not to mention your kids will love to hang out with you at work. Let's hope that you did not start in a career that averages $2 an hour as the norm?

Strategy is planning and is one of the steps to becoming a professional driver. The driver that does not plan does not have a successful career. You should be planning everything you do, you should be planning on delays, and you should be planning for running profitable. I have seen drivers do everything from try to stay out longer so they don't have to do a certain run to running certain areas for prestige like California. It may feel good to tell someone you run California and you are a big time trucker, but if you're not making any money what is the point. The successful drivers I know running California have it down to a science, they plan their trips.

Here are some tips to help you plan your week. Always deliver your first load of the week on Mondays if possible. Arrive at your destination the night before so you are fresh and have hours to run the next day. Aim to put in five hundred miles a day for five consecutive days; your goal is 2500 miles per week. Calculate your border crossings and delivery income to maximize efficiency. Don't go home during the week unless absolutely necessary. Better to stay in work mode and get the job done, it can be hard to go back to work after being home most of the day. Plan out your time, miles per month, miles per week, and miles per day and be consistent, If you can do that you will go a long way to giving yourself a raise as a professional truck driver. Good luck with the planning and I hope if I see you at McDonald's you are in line to buy a hamburger.

In addition to planning your days you need to plan on your business growing. The best way to do that is to look for opportunities as they arise to make your business better like dedicated runs, opportunities for new areas and more. Remember keeping steady income running through your business is key.

He got the call from his boss, we have a load of squid going to Newfoundland, do you want to take it? Never been to Newfoundland before, and after quickly navigating through his calendar in his head he said yes. he had been getting deeply bored in the run he was doing and this would be a great way changing things up and seeing some different scenery. This sounded like a sweet deal, meet a driver coming out of the East Coast of the United States, pick up his trailer and head off to Newfoundland. The trick would be catching the boat as they only arrive in eight hour shifts. He was told he would be reloading out of the same place on the island with a load for Moncton, New Brunswick. No problem he thought. As it turned out the trip wasn't quite that easy, and he found out why many drivers don't like to run to Newfoundland. For most it is about the miles, the time, and the boat arrival can throw your whole week out of whack. He learned this the hard way. Arriving at the dock although he was early, due to the tourists they pushed him back eight hours for another boat. When arriving in Newfoundland the load wouldn't be ready until the next day, he offered to stay but they pulled him home empty. The whole trip was a learning experience and he can now say he had been there. The most compelling thing after the moose was the total beauty of the landscape, this made it all worth while. The reason I tell you this story was to show you that taking a chance may be an advantage for you.

As companies buy newer equipment, change runs across the country, and acquire new clients many opportunities can arise that may move your business to the next level. For instance a carrier I deal with just came into acquiring some refrigerated units to haul produce or other temperature controlled produce within their fleet. If you are asked to take a load or are offered the opportunity to work with those trailers, you can be afraid of the opportunity and turn down the offer, or you can look into all the facts of how they plan to operate, check out how much it may benefit your mileage or fuel operation and take a chance. It could lead to things like steady freight, prime loading situations, and give you an elevated position in the company. If nothing else it may help you change your normal routine and add some spice to your position. Some people are afraid of opportunities and stay back to see what happens, many times leaving them at the back of the pack. Sometimes by going in early you get some hick ups, but you also have a chance to streamline the work and make it better by being a leader. Only you know which type of person you are.

Dedicated runs are great for keeping steady income coming through your business but have the deadly habit of creating a boring environment and landing you into whirlwind position that is not very good for business.

So you're driving along on the same run you do every week, the sun is shining, the roads are clear, and you know the destination and route so well you could drive there with your eyes closed. You've been doing this for five years straight and it is starting to get stale. You're making good money, the miles are steady, and the work is relaxed. Inside you are starting to get restless however, looking for something new to grab your attention. The problem is you have been performing well on this route and the company wants you to stay on it, the question is for how long? I have had dedicated work most of my career as a driver and have always made good money doing so. The trouble is that it can be hard to get off them or change the program once they start. If a company is not in tune with the drivers on dedicated runs they can find out the hard way when the drivers quit and they don't understand why.

This happens to many drivers as they go thorough their careers. It certainly happened to me and caused a shift in direction. It is quite ironic actually, as drivers moving through our careers we spend most of or time with a company trying to get steady miles. Balancing the job with personal time has always been a struggle in this industry and those that have found that balance have made some hard decisions. Since we are all paid by the mile for the most part it can be very rewarding to be offered a steady run with guaranteed miles. This gives you money and miles you can depend on with lanes you are familiar with making your job and personal life much easier to plan. There is one problem with this model, boredom! It is very easy to get bored on dedicated runs if you don't have some plan in place to keep things fresh. Much of this can be discussed at the beginning of signing on for such work so that everyones understands the best way to work with the dedicated program.

When offered a dedicated run, note that as a check mark on your resume. Not everyone is offered a run like that and it means you are a leader, do things properly, and have a good track record of being reliable, so this is a good feather in your cap. Although many of us focus on the positive parts of being awarded a run like that, there are some negative areas that should be addressed. Make sure you have some type of relief for the run should you be ill, on vacation, or need time off. Make sure yourself and the relief driver have the same mindset and service philosophy so that your service level won't be brought down by someone else's bad judgment. Arrange to be able to take a week on the open board or other run at least every two months to keep yourself fresh and a change from going to the same destination all the time. Keep communication levels open with dispatch and other operational staff with customer feedback. Some of these may change based on the runs, but are things to look for when signing on to dedicated service. Boredom can set in after a while and can be very problematic if not addressed. Keeping aware of the problem will help you with the solutions.

Managing your income and expenses are one piece of the puzzle to a successful business, but there is one other piece that is even more important than the others, something that can make or break the whole business, that's you! Burn out is a real reality in the transportation business and when you're an Owner Operator trying to keep all the balls in the air like a juggling clown you can over-do it and do serious damage to your health. We need you to help drive your success.

Many of us get into this industry and feel we are professional because we hold that special license, drive that big shiny truck, or have been brought up through the industry ranks by a family member or friend. In the old days that was enough, right? Hey, the saying was if you can shift gears you were good to go, however the industry isn't that way anymore. Today it is a totally different beast especially as an owner operator. You're not only a truck driver, but a regulations expert, a financial officer, a business owner, a bookkeeper, an accountant, a maintenance person, wash attendant and more.

So how do you juggle all of that, be successful, and have a life. You can't. Why, because your human and that's okay. So let's get you on the right track, if you're a driver, let's make the new year the year for you. If you're an owner operator it should be a year of growth for you.

Divide the number of miles you ran in a year by the weeks you've worked. If you were around 2500 miles per week then you're pretty good. Now think about the time you spent on the road. Was it used wisely? How can you make more money, gain more personal time or run smarter? Maybe it's time to change lanes and try on a new run, or change the way you manage your time. Take time to evaluate where you career is going and you'll find a new voice to guide you to a new career focus. Now if you're an owner operator you have an additional focus, you have a business. Being an owner operator takes the job of truck driver to a whole new level. There was enough stress as a driver but now you have to be a business owner, manager etc. It can be overwhelming. As an owner operator you need to have all areas of your business under control. So if you're an owner operator follow the same steps as a driver but the real benefit is looking into your operation to increase your profits. Are you running as profitable as you should be?

Most drivers run without any kind of a plan. You know what they say "if you don't plan to succeed then you're planning to fail". I'm not sure who said that but it is very true. Many drivers feel if they ask for help or don't come across as knowing everything they're a failure. Nothing could be further from the truth.

A business is a giant undertaking for anybody. Let's make you profitable, let's give you a raise. What if we increased your wages by say 2%? Let's use some hard numbers; 2,500 miles a week for 50 weeks, after all you need a vacation! That comes to 125,000 a year. Let's assume you're making $1.05/mile to give you $131,250.00 a year. Let's assume with some proper business consulting, bookkeeping and accounting we save you 2% of your earnings. You would have saved $2,625.00. Now, if you saved that money what could it do for you? Is that a truck payment or two, a mortgage payment on your house or a new set of tires for the truck? What if you squeezed out 5%, 10% or more? How many of you are setup as an incorporated company, yet running your business as a sole proprietor. How much money are you losing per year, per month or per mile? How do you save that kind of money?

Time means everything in trucking however, and having good time management skills go along way to making or breaking the bank. In the business world time is money or so it is said. If you are wasting time you are wasting productivity therefore you are wasting money. That holds true for many of us in business or not. It's all around us as well, just watch people as they rush around all day trying to catch up with this or trying to complete that. If you really want to tick them off ask them to complete a task for you by a certain time, and watch the fireworks go. Now some people don't feel that time management can work for them. The excuses I get are that, "too many outside factors affect my time frame", or "I am paid to work here for eight hours anyway". Those situations may be true but that doesn't mean you can't be productive within that time frame. The group that probably needs time management the most but refuses to use it is the truck drivers of world. As I speak with owner operators across the country through seminars and workshops I hear the same thing, "Dispatch doesn't give us the time we need" or "we can't make any money!" That may be true but are you doing the things that are important for your business to be successful by using time wisely? Only you can control your time and if you're losing miles because of bad time management then no one can be blamed for result in your business. Every moment counts so use them wisely.

We are talking about the professional driver here and there is certain situations that you will come across that will affect your time. Those outside forces are necessarily under anyone's control as they may be weather or traffic related. You also have hours of service which tell you how much work you can put in during the day and so on. But as an owner operator you need to keep your eye on the profit and loss of your business and also future stability of the business through productivity. Many owner operators feel they don't have to work hard or can schedule time off whenever they want, but that isn't true as those wheels need to keep moving. So how do you plan for all of the unknown factors that affect your schedule?

The first part is to know your break-even point for the business on a monthly basis. This will be based on the budget you created when starting your operation as an owner operator. How much work do you need? The next step is to make sure you know how much profit you want to make above your costs, is it 5%, 10%, or 20%. Now break your mileage in to the days you have available to work. So let's say you need to complete 500 miles per day to create the income you want for your business. Your going to lose a certain amount of time unloading, loading, clearing customs, etc so that needs to be factored in to your calculations. If you are waiting to be unloaded for an hour that should be replacing the income for that driving time being lost. So as you factor in all of those situations you will be evaluating your operation to make sure each day you are making the money you have set out to make. Now let's assume you are working in Canada and have 13 hours of driving time available to put in the miles. Five hundred miles will take approximately 10 hours of driving time. Factor in your breaks and inspections and you should require around 12 hours a day without any major delays. So set your daily limit at 12 hours and you have a safety net of an hour. Just because you can run 13 hours a day doesn't mean you should. If you are trip planning effectively and managing your time, while watching your business you will find you are more productive with less time. You can also increase your profits by keeping your finger on the pulse of your business. Manage your time effectively on and off duty and you will succeed at time management. Remember time is money!

He throws one more popcorn into his mouth to finish the bowl. One last touchdown and the game is over. As the crowd roars to an exciting finish, he decides he better get going, after all he should be in Chicago sometime in the morning. He could run all night no problem. Leaving at 7:00pm for the run made sense in his mind, because to him his weekend was the most important thing on his mind. Dispatch told him to be in there by 8am, but hey they always say that and he's been late before. As a long term employee he has stopped trying to prove himself, they should know him by now. As he rolls into the customer location after a rather busy night of driving he is haggard and worn. Thinking to himself not too bad, he was only an hour late and backs in to unload. The customer is a little upset as they were waiting for that product. He decides to let dispatch handle it over the phone and walks out.

This happens to many of us especially as we gain more experience. The thought process that we can still make our destination after leaving later and later can be a real problem with drivers not understanding the importance of customer service and how it affects the company. Many bids and proposals for freight have time lines built into them to ensure good service. This is a benchmark that can affect other proposals down the road for future freight and locations. With a large amount of transportation companies around getting sound contracts can be a feat in itself. Ask your top level management what goes on in the board room with these companies and you will get a whole new perspective on how freight contracts are awarded. They don't just fall in your lap like most people think. It is usually hours of back room meetings and negotiations before the freight is awarded to a carrier. So arriving late for customer deliveries, and assuming that another excuse will get you out of the hot seat might need some rethinking.

As a driver what can you do to improve your performance? The easiest thing to do is to make sure you are operating to the best of your abilities. Arriving on time for pickups and deliveries, managing your hours of service to the maximum allowed, and taking pride in your equipment are the best ways to improve your performance. Think like the business owner, take ownership of your trip as though this was your company. It will bring you to a whole new level in becoming a professional driver.

Jim was in a hurry, he had done his best to beat all the barriers that he could think of to avoid delays on his route, he left early, he stayed off the main roadways that were continually congested, and he planned for his breaks and fuel. He had done a good job, what he didn't plan for was a freak accident on the route that he chose, one that shut the roadway down for over an hour. Should he panic, should he start getting upset and fly off the handle? None of that will change the situation and will not help to make things go any faster, so he makes the dreaded call to dispatch about his delay. He then begins to sit and wait.

Remember those days when traffic had a certain pattern to it? You could leave after a certain time (better known as after traffic) and you would have a clear run through the city. You could pin point certain days when traffic would be light and roads would be empty. That's the reason so many drivers liked driving at night because the traffic is much lighter. That works for the most part but in my years of driving experience even that plan is not fool proof. Have you ever arrived in Chicago or Toronto at 2 o'clock in the morning to find the highway lit up with lights and traffic at a full stop? As things change with people working from home and coffee shops more, population growth cause more people to be out and about on the roadways those traffic patterns we knew so well are slowly starting to erode away. The industry however is going the opposite way by trying to get more people on the roads in the way of owner operators and drivers so more trucks are needed. So how does this affect you as a professional driver?

The first part is to remember that you are a "Professional Driver" and that you have no control over those areas outside of your personal control. Once you have completed as much planning as possible to make sure your trip is safe and timely you have done your part. The rest of your duties are to make sure you drive safe.

The first part is to remember that you are a "Professional Driver" and that you have no control over those areas outside of your personal control. Once you have completed as much planning as possible to make sure your trip is safe and timely you have done your part. The rest of your duties are to make sure you drive safe. Part of driving safe is keeping your cool and keeping your patience level on high alert. Everyone keeps cool in different ways, I myself hate traffic and do my best to avoid it at all costs. To me that means leaving earlier than needed to make sure I have enough time and am relaxed on my arrival. Other drivers don't mind traffic and probably have their own ways of staying cool. Remember being cool, and I am not talking about wearing sun glasses at night is vital for the safety of the public and your health as a driver. Medical issues can be created from finding yourself uptight in traffic, or worse getting road rage. Being cool means recognizing the situations that get you uptight and finding ways to avoid those issues. Being cool is being professional-that's where you come in!

"You don't need that stuff! It's just holding us up!" yelled the dock worker. The driver kept to his work as if not to hear the man yelling in the background. To him it was important, it meant pride in his load, excellent customer service, ownership of his position, the difference between mediocre and outstanding, it meant he was organized, he placed the plywood in between the skids as the forklift set in the final piece. He strapped the rear of the load and proceeded to count and sign off the paper work. The shipper becoming more impatient by the moment and was already starting to get the next driver lined up to back into the dock. To the shipper it was all about finishing at 4:00pm. To the owner operator who had just loaded the freight it meant the difference between a damage claim and a profitable run. The freight was now in his control and as far as he was concerned this was now his own customer.

How many of you have run across this situation out on the road? In my 25 years of driving I have seen this many times. To most shippers it is all about getting the freight out the door so they can go on break, or go home at the end of their shift. Some places you are not even allowed to watch the shipper load your truck. But when you think of if who is responsible for that load once it leaves the dock. I can tell you it is not the shipper. Even worse if it is loaded improperly it can cause everything from damage to overweight fines, to possibly death in the event of a crash or rollover. Even if you make it safely to the customer's door if the freight is all over the floor what does that do for your company's customer service or insurance record.

The truth is organization and being orderly starts with you. How you set up your truck from the beginning, the type of equipment you carry and so forth all shows the shipper and receivers the type of driver you are and how much you care. Now some operations it may be harder to do, but for many especially those that are running dedicated equipment this shouldn't be a problem. Carrying things like plywood on your truck, extra straps and load bars all go a long way to being a successful driver. It is your right to know what is inside your trailer and how it is loaded; in fact it is your responsibility.

So what can you do when arriving at shippers to make sure you are loaded properly? The first thing is to have a well organized trailer from the time you back into the dock. Ask to watch the load loaded and count the pieces going on the truck. Educate the shipper on the type of equipment that you have and the best way to load it for maximum weight. A 10 foot one inch axle spread is loaded completely different to a tandem dry van trailer. Secure your cargo even if the shipper doesn't feel it will move on you, it will! Finally confirm your piece count and if you can't sign the bill of lading stating count unconfirmed by driver and have the trailer sealed. If you just sign what is there you are now responsible if the freight count is short at the other end. Being an organized driver is up to you and may seem like more work right now, but in the end your career and pocket book will be better off for it.

He was sitting in line for what seemed like a life time. Inching forward almost on the hour ruined the decent trip time he was making before on the trip had come to a halt. So far it had been two hours and he was still only halfway across the bridge. Out of a lack of boredom and trying to make use of his valuable time Tom began to look around the truck at things he could do. He thought of cleaning the cab, but in a customs line up that may start to look a little suspicious. He could have played a video game but Wi-Fi was not available in this area. So he broke down and selected paperwork, not his first choice, but probably the wisest of the three. Pulling out his paperwork and using his table board made for the steering wheel he began to complete his trip sheet with receipts and load information. As the line inched forward even more, things began to move along a little faster it even got to the point where it was moving along by the minute. Not paying attention a paper he was working on fell onto the floor, Tom leaned over to pick it up, but as he did he didn't realize his foot let pressure off of the brake pedal. Everything happened in an instant. The truck rolled ahead, bouncing off of the rear end of the truck ahead. Even at the low speed of the roll the damage was substantial. Tom could not believe what had happened. He now had to call his company and tell them what happened. At least the trailer ahead of him wasn't damaged, but the new grill and bumper would be expensive, not to mention the bruise to his ego. Tom had been one of the most respected drivers in the fleet, how could he make such a mistake?

As a professional driver it is important to use your time wisely and situations like waiting at customs, waiting for loads at shippers, or waiting to get unloaded are all great times to multi-task and get ahead on paperwork and other house keeping duties, however it has to be done safely. Securing the vehicle from moving should be the first item to be taking care of when attempting to multi-task in moving environment. The situation that happened to Tom is not new, it has happened to many good professional drivers over time. It is usually the small mistakes that eat away at drivers over the years. Many of us see the potential for large incidents to happen. Things like getting into an accident in a customs lineup doesn't even enter our mind, however I know many drivers that it has happened to. Brake pedals and air systems rely on a certain amount of pressure to keep them locked. If that pressure is released even in the slightest it can release enough pressure to move. Sometimes being professional starts with the little mistakes, not the big ones.

John bought a truck and felt confident going into business on his own. He thought he had done everything right, he researched the different elements of becoming an Owner Operator, he looked into a variety of options and was happy with the carrier he was with. He thought he had it all together. Now that he owned the truck the big thing for him was to make up for lost time and keep the wheels rolling. As with any business starting up and raising capital can be difficult and some hard work is needed in the beginning to catch up with the cash outlay required in the beginning. As you go along however you realize you are having a hard time catching up with paperwork, and other duties because you are running all the time. As you move further along it gets harder and harder to catch until you get so overwhelmed that you lose control of your operation. This happens to many Owner Operators and they get so far behind that they begin hurting themselves and their business. So how do you keep yourself from becoming so much in trouble that you can't keep up, planning!

Planning is the key to everything, a business plan should have been made up before buying a truck, you should have a plan for growth, a plan for operating your business, and a plan for keeping the wheels turning. Many Owner Operators focus on the wheels turning part and forget the rest. That is where they keep going wrong. The rest of the puzzle is just as important to keep the wheels going, you need to submit your receipts in a certain time period, government filings need to be completed regularly and so forth. That doesn't even include just having your operation run smoothly by being on top of your costs and income. Cash flow is key in business and those that know where their money is going will be the winners of the game. So if you're falling behind how do you stop the trail and get back on track, how do you catch up and refocus on your game plan?

As mentioned earlier most Owner Operators are focused on keeping the wheels turning and they should be, however if you are so far behind on keeping track of your operation it may be costing you more money than it's worth. Lets say you are making a dollar a mile and you can run five hundred miles in a day. If you are far behind on your operational tasks you may losing money in things like HST filings that can give you much needed cash, cost analysis that can help you save money in your operation therefore putting more cash in your business. I have seen drivers that do not do their tax filings on time and are owed thousands of dollars of much needed cash, but they will keep running up and down the road to make five hundred bucks. That doesn't make sense! You would be better to take a day or so off and clean up your operation. If you are to far gone it might be better to hire someone to help with that program and handle things going forward.

With an organized operation you will find areas that need improvement and make more informed choices for the future. If you don't focus on both the cost and income sides of your business you will find yourself out of business in the future. This is where many Owner Operators go wrong. Take the time to make it right.

It was his third trip this week and he was starting to feel the tiredness setting in. He was used to a couple of trips a week, but this was only Wednesday and he was on the third short trip. Having steady work was great and the paycheck would certainly benefit from the healthy miles but his body was feeling the pace. So what was new about this week that hadn't happened in the past? Ted had been running hard and was used to the physical nature of the product he hauled. Tarping, chains, and other job requirements were a way of life for Ted, what he was having trouble with was the emotional side. Personal issues like family and finances were causing Ted some troubled nights and his sleep wasn't as solid as it should have been. It is one thing to lie down for six hours but how many of those are solid sleep hours. As a result Ted was not getting quality sleep and was feeling exhausted.

While driving to the border from his last switch he was starting to fall asleep. He had turned the trip and just had to get to other side of the border before shutting down for the night. He had caught himself drowsing off a couple times on his own but on this particular night he had been caught by someone else, the Police. After the Police officer reviewed his logbook with a fine tooth comb he was released and told to get more rest if he was feeling sleepy. On this trip he managed to get to the other side and shut down.

This happens to many drivers and it comes down to your internal clock and sleep management. As professional drivers the physical part of the job usually is something we are comfortable with and can do without too much thought. We do it everyday and for the most part do it well. This is comfortable level of our positions and we can work for long hours because we are in a comfort zone and can apply a certain amount of pressure to completing the tasks. Where we get caught is the mental part of our brains that add another level above that pressure. Think about the last time that you were driving down the road with a load and started to think about family back home, the work you didn't get done on the weekend, the bills that need to be paid, and other important items in your life. Your work level goes onto autopilot and you begin to focus on the extra pressure. You have now added extra pressure increasing your level of exhaustion. Most of us don't acknowledge that this has happened until we begin to feel tired and don't understand why. So when thinking about your level of exposure to fatigue think about your job as one level and each additional level weighs more on an individual creating a higher exhaustion level. If possible deal with issues so you're not dragging them around with you on the road. Your livelihood depends on it.

Like any other week Tim is running behind again. Leaving late on Sunday and a couple of bad breaks at customer locations has set him back yet again. Tim is a good driver, but time management is not his strong point. As any driver knows that starting the week late won't make things any easier for the rest of the week. As Tim couldn't get his time management act together it was costing him miles and money. As an Owner Operator every mile he missed cost him income from his own pocket. Those lost miles add up at the end of a month and can cause problems with cash flow down the road. Tim just couldn't get moving at the beginning of the week. He wanted more family time and enjoyed tinkering in the work shed on weekends. His health wasn't great, he didn't like exercise or eat well and that seemed to drain energy. He just didn't seem rested when it was time to get going for another week of work.

This is typical of most truck drivers and although not everyone is late many seem to keep that attitude I'll get there when I get there. In a recent article in one of the transportation industry publications there was a study of how road delivery of goods compared to other modes of transportation stood up. Road delivery was still leading the pack with a rough percentage of 82% on time delivery. Higher was courier delivery at 87% and rail and other modes hovered around 70%.

As a professional driver or Owner Operator you may be wondering what that has to do with you. Most of us think we are only one drop in a much larger bucket of water, more like a lake. However we are part of the overall percentage for the industry. Whether you like it or not if you drove a truck for a company in Canada you were part of that survey. Why is that important to you? First it defines the future of your profession. When the Government and other regulatory bodies are looking to install rail lines, do away with certain modes of transportation or expand others we are showing them that road delivery is a reliable way of getting consumers their goods. That's what keeps many companies in the transportation game, which in turn keeps you employed. Most Owner Operators and drivers don't realize that what they do plays a larger part in our industry. As with anything a large group starts with just one person so improving your own work flow is one of the best things you can do for your own business and the industry as a whole. Helping the industry will help you at the same time.

We all know that every truck or vehicle for that matter needs the proper tires, axles, and frame to support the products you haul with your truck. Proper axle and frame configuration is important to the support system for your truck. If the tires are quality and well maintained they will hold up under the loads the truck will be required to carry over the years. Anyone who has been trucking for any length of time knows how important proper tires are for your truck. What I want you to look at is the support system for your career, have you given it the same importance as you put onto the frame, axles, and tires of your truck? Think about how many tire pieces you see on the roadways in the summer months. Those come from a variety of issues such as reused tires, under inflated tires, and increased heat exposure, among other problems. By taking care of those items on a regular basis the support system of your vehicle will stay in strong shape.

Now lets take a look at the support system for your career. You need the same components as the truck, frame, axles, and tires. Think of your career foundation being the frame, this may be your family, your values, your heritage, this might be the reason you got into trucking in the first place, maybe the reason you stay in trucking. The next part of your support system are the axles. The axles would take place as the experience you have, career goals, training in the transportation industry, any achievements and awards you've won. Once the axles are in place you have the tires. The tires of your career are your employer, your business if you're an Owner Operator. It may be the type of specialty service you're in or the products and services you haul. To have a successful career you need to have all these components in place and operating well at the same time. Much like the preventive maintenance on your vehicle your career may need preventive maintenance once in a while. Is that frame support strong, is your family life balanced with your career and in good condition? Now take a look at your axle configuration, are they set to where you are getting the most bang for the buck?

Do you have goals moving you forward in life or are you just going through the motions? I see people all over our industry and many fall into two categories. Some don't have enough training and others have too much training and are not using it to the best of their abilities. Maybe your experience can give your career a shot up the ladder. Now we all know how important air pressure is to our tires and longevity. The same goes for your tire preparation in your career. Are you working for a decent company or is it time for a change. Is your business operating profitably or do you need some outside eyes to take a look at the situation and help make some decisions? These are all important components that need to work together, but also require their own maintenance and upkeep. So if you are rolling down the highway and the truck just doesn't feel right to you, you may have a tire problem or greater problem if with the axles and frame. The same holds true for your career, if the road seems bumpy, if the frame and axles are good, maybe you need to work on the tire pressure? When it all comes together you will have a smooth ride.

Taking Advantage of New Technology

Remember the old days, a C.B. in the truck, a pillow for the jump seat, and pair of sunglasses and you were ready to drive on down the road. Those were the early days when sleepers weren't even common and trucking was a hard job to handle. As trucks got better equipment to go with them got better giving us luxurious sleepers, satellite television and more. I remember watching television on my little 10 inch portable television at the truck stop. I think I got one channel and if you were in a place like Southern Kentucky the big news was how big the deer was that the local hunter caught, a traffic report was out of the question. Things have changed since those days and there have been great developments in order to keep drivers efficient and on time. If you ask some they will tell you that the best thing to do is go out and buy the latest gizmo and you will be all set. That may be true in some cases, but if you are not ready to use that type of technology then it is just a waste of money. Technology is great if you use it and a waste if you don't, so don't buy what you don't need. So how do you choose technology that will be helpful to you among all of the ads about the latest products? Through the use of a pen and paper and a little brainstorming on how you would use it.

The first thing is to figure out is what you need or what would improve the way you're doing things now. Make sure you take a look at your costs in the way you have things working. For example when I was on the road full time my big thing was to call home every night from where ever I was to talk with my family. Back then there were no cell phones in trucks so I purchased an 800 number for my home phone so I could call without the expense of a large phone bill. Today there are much better options such as Skype and so on that are absolutely free. So write down things you like to do personally such as movies, your accounting, staying in touch with family, tracking your business and trips, games etc. Now write down things that can help you do your job better, such as a phone that can double as an EOBR for your logbook, or GPS for trip planning. Look for ways to do the things you do now even easier. Once you have all of that in hand take a look at what is available to you cost wise, and what the company may be supplying to you.

The goal is to get as much out of one machine as possible so you don't have to take along too many items. With all of the applications out there these days you should be able to find something user friendly for yourself. Before buying take a look at what is coming out over the horizon for example Apple usually puts out updated products around late summer and Christmas so you may want to wait if you are close to those times and get the latest software. The point is to improve your efficiency and the best way to do that is to streamline your own process by using technology that is efficient. Leave the bells and whistles out if you don't need them.

If you are new to the industry you may not realize what all the commotion is about with EOBRS. EOBR stands for Electronic On Board Recorders. At this point they come in a variety of different styles from equipment that looks like a laptop computer to cell phones. Many companies have already gone to the recorders and many more will over time. The big stink being raised is that the Government is pushing companies into using them creating a costly expense for the company depending on the version they choose. At first the group targeted were companies with a certain amount of hours of service violations but it seems to be expanding to include everyone. Paper logs are still the industry standard at this time. This isn't meant to debate the use of EOBRs, it is meant to make you aware of how you do your work in the future.

If you are just graduating from a truck school or are looking for a future in the transportation industry this will affect the way you work, your family time, and your business if you decide to become an Owner Operator. The chances of being employed by a carrier using EOBRs is becoming more common. It is likely that you will learn to use them while going through a school program if you haven't been trained already. These machines can do a lot which is why many companies are going to them. They help with compliance issues, they reduce the amount of paper being used, and they have the ability to add more user functions allowing for better time management and delivery times. There is one thing however, that the machines can't do. The machine cannot control your time management. This is why you need to have good time management skills coming into this industry, and this is why there is such an outcry about using them. Those with good time management will learn how to plan their days well and make the most of the hours allowed. Others who are late on regular basis will find it hard to have to stay within the limits of a computer program. On paper many had the chance to adjust records to meet their time frames. With EOBRs the driver had to adjust their time frames to work with the records. Some EOBRs are even set to shut a truck down when they reach their maximum hour allotment. The industry is changing as a whole and the focus is putting the driver as the person responsible for safety and time management.

So for those of you coming into the industry I caution you to take a good hard look at yourself and the way you operate. Do you have good time management skills now? If not this is an area to be improved and should be a focus for you. Without good time management skills you will find that you have a hard time keeping up with the transportation industry and its many changes.

Social media has become one of the true wonders of the world and it can be used for both good and bad. The idea of social media is to be, well social, but this can lead to all sorts of problems if not handled in a timely manner. In the old days word of mouth spread one person at a time; today it spreads by the thousands at a time. That can be bad if the message is negative that is going out, and can be great if people are speaking positively about your company. Of course how will you know if you are not on the platform? Many companies restrict people from being on social media at work, however at lunch hours with the multitude of cell phones and tablets people don't need your work network to get online. From a management standpoint you need to be on the platform. Even if you don't plan to participate go on once in a while and check what is being said about your company. If you are a recruiter then this should be one of your reference areas to check up on a new driver. If they have posted it then you are allowed to view it, and many do. As an Owner Operator you can join groups on social media to fill that lonely void of being on the road. Social media can be used to help get a company message out to thousands of potential drivers, but it can also be used to keep watch those interested in applying to the company. If they found you online then they are online. So how do you use the platform to your advantage?

First create some guidelines about what will be considered a problematic issue, what topics will raise a red flag with your company, and what topics are totally unacceptable. The platforms may have their own guidelines but you should have your own company standard. Create a list of actions to be taken should you find one of those offenses occurring online.

Now create a system for monitoring the platforms to see what is being said. There are many ways of doing this on the platforms themselves such as changing your settings to be notified by email of any comments made about your company, etc. Look under privacy setting under most of the platforms. Now you can monitor comments and be able to keep an eye on the employees, you can also type in their names to see if they have signed up and read their walls. Be careful not to abuse your power or someone else's rights.

For new or potential drivers make sure you check them out with social media. It will give you a true picture of the type of people they are away from work. The reason is that many people on social media forget that they are on the internet so they let their hair down. Don't comment, just monitor! The point is if you are hiring this person you may have to have a discussion before signing them on about company culture, etc. If they are not doing anything wrong you can get to know them and can mention their family or hobbies in the interview. This will give them a little nudge to let them know you keep an eye on the platform informing them to watch their comments. Social media is a great thing in more ways than one, but like everything else every great thing can cause additional problems. Make sure you know who or what your problems are!

With social media becoming the hottest thing on the planet at this time you may wonder what all the hype is about if you don't understand how the different platforms work. So lets take a look at one and how it can help you. Twitter is a platform that I think is very effective just because of the way it was developed. Many of the other platforms are created to engage with other people, share stories and pictures, and to connect with people that you may not see on a daily basis. That is great if that is your goal, but for some of us keeping on top of information, checking top breaking stories and more is the reason for using social media. That's where Twitter comes in with a bang.

Twitter is set up to let you follow people, organizations, news feeds, and specific industries of your choice. The nice thing is that you can follow people and not have to communicate with them if you choose not to. Due to the fact that Twitter only allows you one hundred and forty characters in the message line much of the information is formulated from another source such as a blog. For that reason alone I find Twitter much more effective than some of the other platforms. As the other platforms force you to send short irrelevant messages because each communication can turn into a discussion Twitter brings in feeds from the organization itself therefore allowing people to follow based on content instead of thread discussion. For that reason alone is a good reason to use Twitter.

So why is Twitter good for the transportation industry and how should you set it up for your team? First inform your team that the company is now on Twitter. Decide on the information that you want to send out or receive whether it be safety, general transportation information, regulations, etc. Don't send anything too delicate over social media, remember the whole world is watching. You can also follow organizations that can help you perform better such as the Border Crossing Agency, State Traffic Departments and more.

The idea is to customize your company Twitter account to benefit you specifically not just use it for silly messages. Sending out information in this form has other benefits. For instance safety messages are best sent out in short forms instead of giant lengthy volumes. It has been proven that people take in the information more readily when given in short doses. So you could send out a safety message every week for your team. That information can also be "retweeted" (a Twitter term for sharing a message) to other people on the Twitter platform. A nice fact about Twitter is that it can be checked quickly. Items can be scrolled though or read in depth allowing people to check the platform on a regular basis. With smart phones many people have the Twitter application on their phones allowing messages to be retrieved automatically.

So Try Twitter and see if there is a fit for you. Ask at your next safety meeting how many people are on the platform and you be surprised how many of your team are already involved. Increase your efficiency by watching border crossings, traffic patterns, industry regulations and more. Information like that can keep you running profitably for years to come.

Have you been working too much? As an entrepreneur or business owner it is very easy to get into the trap of working all the time without a break, you have to eat, so letting up makes business nerve racking for the future. The importance of taking time off cannot be underestimated however, and may even be the difference in how your business grows. I recently took a vacation with my wife to the Caribbean for some much needed away time. It was the first vacation that I had last year and it was long overdue. We were celebrating a special occasion so we had decided on going away last year in September. Although I checked email and phone messages on a daily basis I tried to stay away from work all together. I brought just my iPhone, no laptop, etc.

What people don't realize is that the vacation can be the most important thing you can do for yourself and your business. It doesn't have to be to the Caribbean, just some time off to recharge the brain cells. What normally happens with me is that I am working or maybe I should say working on me. With no daily work to take care of you give your mind a chance to relax and absorb your surroundings. You will find that you start thinking about the bigger picture and where you would like to take your business in the future. The small details will vanish for the most part. You need to relax your mind on a regular basis. One thing you notice as the clientele in your business grows is that you will find that more work is done in relaxed settings such as golf courses, entertainment venues and so on. That is because the people attending are higher up in their businesses and are spending more time working on their business as opposed to in their businesses. For example last year I started golfing and have noticed a big difference in some of the relationships that I have formed while on the golf course. I can't explain it but it works.

So the moral of the story is take time on a regular basis to recharge the brain, get more involved in some of the leisure activities that go with business and you will see your business grow. It may surprise you how fast this can work for you. Schedule vacation time on a regular basis, even if you stay home and don't answer the phone.

Aging is certainly something all of us will or have gone through as life goes on. Taking time to recharge through our work lives helps some people grow gracefully. Many of us however are stuck in our ways and that sometimes can be bad for business. Aging is a funny thing, it gives you life experiences, self awareness, and your own opinion. Some people over time can still see the light beyond the tunnel and others just don't have the foresight to do that anymore. We usually call this "set in your ways" as a term from not reaching or trying to see through to the future. I know many people like that and continue to see others move in that direction, but I ask you to look at yourself and see if you are set in your ways? You may be asking yourself why this is important to look at, after all you don't plan on changing, you're set in your ways! It can be the difference between career advancement to a successful lifestyle. Many people that close their minds to different opportunities lose some great opportunities because of close minded thinking. So why do you need to be open minded to be a truck driver?

Just the other day I attended an event that has been going on for a long time and that many of you have been a part of in the past, the Fergus Truck Show. This annual event in it's hey day was renowned as the largest truck show in Canada at one time. Today it has been struggling even though it has passed the 25 year mark. I think what happened to the show is it got so big and set in the way they were doing things that they lost some great people and it focused on the wrong parts of trying to bring people through the gates. For this show to bounce back from dismal years they will have to refocus on what the show really is, a truck show, and get the trucks back. This will have to be done by people willing to get out of their own way and listen to the feedback of those attending.

For those of you that wonder how this relates to the show, it is the same thing. If your position is getting stale, or you are beginning to be frustrated with your job, then it might be time to get out of your own way and make the job fun again. Think back to what sparked your excitement in the beginning? Was it the trucks, the runs, maybe it's time to change. Like the truck show change may take time and may be hard but it can be done, it just takes effort.

How do you change? Start with yourself, are you open to other opinions, are you willing to take a chance and trust your instincts? If so you are heading on the right road to keeping yourself energized and youthful. Maybe take on a new run, spruce up the truck again, attend a truck show for some new ideas, just get back in the saddle and create that energy. You'll be glad you did!

Have you met Joe? Joe is a very experienced driver, has 30 years of experience in the industry, has seen it all on his travels from coast to coast, and has made a decent living as a professional truck driver. His company has given him his choice of runs because he is good at what he does, he is driving top notch equipment rarely older than two years old, and has been a star driver for the company. He may be sitting across from you right now in the coffee shop. You can see him, he has that tired look, his routine so ordinary he doesn't even look at the menu anymore to order his meal. He's stopped talking to many of his colleagues other than to say hello because he has heard all their whining before. Joe is the guy starting to rust.

On a vehicle you can see the rust, once it starts it can take over a vehicle in a quick matter of time. Just leave it unattended and you can see it engulf the vehicle and you will wonder how it started. Rust usually starts in areas that we don't see, under wheel wells, in dark corners and other areas not so noticeable. When we do start to notice rust on our vehicles we can do two things, we can tackle it and keep it from growing, or we can leave it alone and let it take its course. Many times unless the vehicle is the pride and joy of the owner the rust will be left alone with the tag line, "She's an old girl anyway." A little longer and the rust will eventually take over the vehicle.

The same works with our careers, rust in our careers takes on the form of boredom, of complacency, and your career can suffer greatly if not looked after. Remember when you started your career, it was exciting, you learned new things, you went new places, and you met new people. You moved up in your career through getting new equipment, going to more money, and getting better runs. You were growing and thriving and you could feel your career moving along in the right direction.

Then it happened, the rust settled in. The first form was when you took that steady run so you could predict your income better. The second was when you received that truck although new, it stopped giving you the excitement level that it used to. Then you got older, you stopped thinking about how to do your job better, you started to go through the motions that you did everyday, the rust grew a little more. You are now Joe, you have been in the position too long, you are afraid to make that change, you are afraid to try something new. There is nothing new for you in the job, everything you look at seems to need a younger outlook so you don't change, you remain the same. The rust takes over until eventually you die, the same as a truck in the field after years of duty, you sit in your rocker the same way, wondering "What if?" The rust has taken over.

The secret to tackling the rust is to keep yourself challenged, keep yourself looking for new opportunities, and keeping yourself growing mentally. Many have gone on to bigger and better things, they have battled the rust. You don't have to change careers, you just have to keep learning something new, keep the excitement in your career and you will keep the rust away.

Running by the Mile - 10 Steps to a Successful Trucking Business

Step 8

Saving Money as an Owner Operator

Business is one of those things in life that go up and down. One minute you are on top of the world and the next you are rolling on the ground. That's why when people go spouting how much they grossed in their business, I laugh and ask for the real numbers. The real question is what is the profit margin for your business after you paid yourself and your bills? Depending on the business you're in the fourth year can cripple your business. Here's why!

Part of the problem is expectation, when you were starting up your career you were excited to get under way. You've bought a truck, managed to sign on with a carrier and are now your own boss. That first year you may still be learning how to read the map to your destination, or maybe crossing the border is your biggest challenge. No one is expecting you to earn money, it's your first year you're allowed to fail.

Year two you start getting into your own. You've messed up but are still holding on and trying to pay the bills based on how they land in your lap. You're starting to get the truck driving part down and look to being comfortable in the seat as a professional driver. Getting those miles is the most important part of your program because if you get enough miles you will be able to catch up on some bills and put money away.

Year three starts to hit you hard. The truck requires a little more maintenance, you're thinking about trading it in but you need to keep it another year or so yet. You start to worry that you have not set a side enough for maintenance, in fact you haven't set anything aside for maintenance. You've finally caught up on your taxes but need to start running the truck more like a business. You realize that but are behind and just trying to stay on top of it all.

Then year four hits you. You need to replace the truck. You realize that you should have incorporated due to your tax situation, and your cash flow is starting to run low. You begin to look for help but is it too late?

This is a common scenario with many people in business especially owner operators. As I coach many of my clients I try to set them up properly in year one. The problem is many don't feel that the financial side of their business is important as they just want to get down the road. When I talk to them later they wish they had listened to me, but is it too late? Year four in most businesses is when everything comes to a halt. If you're prepared for it and have listened to quality advice you will go through it and come out successful on the other end. It is important to put your processes in place early on so that when things start to affect your business you are able to handle them. If not you will find that you are struggling to keep alive. If you haven't done so already it is important that you start doing things right today. Hire someone to have a look at your business and report on what they see then make a goal and start correcting those issues. I have seen Owner Operators that have made it to ten and twelve years suddenly go bankrupt. Eventually poor operational decisions will eat away at your business, planning for those early on is the key to success.

As you know it doesn't matter how many bells and whistles you add to your truck without the most important part, the truck it will not move one inch. The engine in your truck is the most important component of the truck and without it you have nothing. So when you buy a truck some of the information you require to make a sound decision is life history, miles acquired, wear and tear analysis, oil samples, and so on to make sure your engine will last you for the time that you need to get out of it. This information along with other drive line component information is vital to your success. Once you have decided on a truck usually you would buy some type of warranty as part of your purchase to make sure you are covered if a break down occurs. This my friend is smart buying and good business sense. So lets switch gears a little bit and apply this to your business.

As an Owner Operator you are the engine of your business, take you and your operation out of the business and again you have nothing, you have no business. Like the engine of a truck you are the engine of your business and are required to be in good shape to keep the business running for years to come. You need to look at the components of your business when starting up just like those of a truck. You took a look at the engine oil when buying the truck so you should take a look at your health to make sure it is in good shape, that is your oil sample. You looked at the mileage of your engine and wear and tear so you should look at that in your experience with business and analyze where you may need help. When you finally made the purchase you also took out a warranty to make sure you were protected from a breakdown. You should do the same thing with your business and buy the appropriate insurance coverage. When you were becoming an Owner Operator you looked at certain things before jumping into business, the first being decent equipment, the second being a sound company to lease on with, and the last the commitment to do the job.

Since you have worked hard to get the right truck, don't you think you should work equally hard to create a successful business. You bought decent equipment, leased on with a sound company, and committed to the job. So what do you need for continued success? You will need a decent accountant, a smooth operation, and possibly a business consultant to help you make the right decisions. Adding those components to your business engine will ensure you have a successful career as an Owner Operator.

Don't be one of the many business owners that work hard at the beginning but then let the operation of the business fall down after the initial excitement has gone. You wouldn't spec an engine perfectly to forget to put oil in it down the road, so don't do that to your business engine. Keep improving the profit margin of your business and that will help to keep that excitement level that you had in year one.

Fuel costs are the highest expenses for the owner operator and may even lead the pack in front of payroll and maintenance. Controlling your fuel costs is crucial in making your business a profitable one. On the next few pages we will show you ways to do that so you can have a successful business.

He pulls up to the pump tired and weary needing to energize both he and the truck. His stomach is empty, the fuel tanks are empty, and his energy is draining as the week of miles closes to an end. It has been a hard week and he is completing the last run and heading for home. As he does every other day, he removes the cap to the fuel tank and starts pumping. The spinning of the gauges going around are moving so fast they are almost hypnotic. He fills one tank, then the other until both are full, this has become as familiar as eating breakfast in the morning. He continues inside to pay for the fuel with the company fuel card, although he is shown the total it doesn't register. He is more interested in having a shower and something to eat than how much the fuel cost him. He signs the paper, grabs the towel from the counter and walks down the hall, shoving the fuel receipt in his pocket.

In my 25 years of experience on the road almost 90% or the drivers and owner operators operate like the example above. Many are using company issued fuel cards accepted across North America and don't know how much fuel they have bought because they just sign for it and it comes off their statements. Unless your company starts telling you which price range or where to fuel it can be hard to know a price guideline to follow. Of course everyone wants the cheapest fuel available, but with transportation the factor of fuel tax and other factors must be weighed before knowing if the place you are buying fuel is really the cheapest for your dollar. As an Owner Operator it is imperative that you know your costs, especially for fuel. Those that wait for the company statement to show the fuel costs are behind the eight ball right off the bat. There are a number of reasons for this, the statements are usually two to four weeks behind the actual purchase so it will be hard to figure out the numbers. Your statement may be wrong, now I know that has never happened, but it could be and that will cause problems in your accounting. What if you were charged too much for the fuel, are you aware of the company discounts? The secret to tracking this type of information is to do it on the side. Keep a notebook with fuel and mileage information and match it to the trips you have run. Not only will this create a backup to help you match your statements, but will also help you know how much fuel your buying. Just because you have pulled up to the pump doesn't mean you have to fill up the truck every time. If cheaper fuel is available down the road, then putting in enough to get you there is good planning. Pretend you are paying cash for your fuel, this will help you pay more attention to your bottom-line and the price you pay at the pump. Just filling up anywhere could be hurting your bottom-line, your fuel tax program, and your pocket book. The smart Owner Operator wins these days.

One of the main expenses on a truck is fuel, it is a variable expense that fleet managers spend most of their waking life figuring out how to control and most drivers don't think about. Talk about being at far ends of the spectrum. Most drivers will use the reasons of sleeping in the truck, keeping it warm while at the truck stop eating and so on as the reasons they idle the truck. In many of the fuel studies it is stated that most trucks are idle and running up to 65 percent of the time. That may be true if you count traffic congestion, border crossings and so forth. Those situations you can't do much about you have to have the truck running. Many times however and we've all seen it many times are the trucks idling while the drivers are inside having a meal. The question is why?

Now I am not a fleet manager so I won't harp on you about shutting off your truck, you're an owner operator you don't have to listen to me, so maybe seeing the cost of idling in numbers may help bring the point home. Assume your truck is getting six miles to the gallon, the price of fuel is roughly $4.00 per gallon and you average 50 miles per hour, you will have used 8.33 gallons of fuel for the hour. That comes to $33 of fuel in money terms. Now reports show that idling a truck for one hour is the same as driving it for two hours. That may or may not be true due to the load weight, road terrain, and so forth. Assume that if you are idling your truck you would use half the fuel used while driving, lets say $15 per hour to average out. With an eight hour break and your truck idling you would come to $120 for the cost of an eight hour break. You get no miles per gallon so you are no further down the road, and we haven't even counted the wear and tear on the engine. Lets say you are five nights out on the road, that makes your idling expense $600 for the week. Again you have gained nothing financially but sending smoke through the pipes. Add that $600 over 50 weeks per year and the number would scare you. As an Owner Operator it is in your best interest to keep your fuel costs down. Staying in motels, buying a generator or other heating system may be more beneficial than idling the truck. Every penny you save adds to your bottom line and thats profits in your company and bank account. Every trip is different, but good time management is one of the most beneficial and lowest cost items that you can do to make business more profitable. Remember watch your bottom line and it will watch you.

Understanding Your Taxes to Save Money

As a business owner it is important that you at least understand the basics of how taxes work as it is a reality of being in business. Now I don't for any instance think or encourage you to take taxes on by yourself, that's why accountants were brought into this world and the world of taxes both personal and business will make you pull your hair out. An accountant for your business is a must, but taxes need to be paid and can greatly affect your bottom line if you don't at least understand the basics of how they work. I am going to generally outline the basic three that will affect the Owner Operator and I encourage the business owner to dig even deeper to learn how you can save money by working your tax situation out to your best advantage.

Realize we all need to pay personal taxes and those are created from your wage, earnings, deductions and so on. Depending on the setup of your business you may be taxed on the amount of money you made from a wage in your business or the total earnings of your business. This is one of the reasons I encourage Owner Operators to become incorporated and take a wage from their company. Personal tax rates are higher than corporate tax rates so you will be taxed on the wage at the personal level, and the company will pay corporate taxes on the rest which are much lower. If you are Sole Proprietor you will pay the personal tax level on the total earnings of your business. The rate goes up over $150,000 where most Owner Operators operate. Talk to an accountant about the tax rate for your business, you may save money by restructuring your business.

The other big tax for businesses is the HST / GST in Canada. This tax is based on products and services bought and sold in the country with the tax rate changing based on the Province. With fuel this will be a big one for the Owner Operator. It is mandatory for businesses making over $30,000 per year and the tax works on a plus minus type of scale.

For instance if you make $100 worth of income plus HST the total (Ontario) would be $113.00. If you bought $80 of fuel and paid HST you would pay $90.40. If you subtract the HST amounts you would have $13-$10.40 =$2.60. When you file your HST return you would have to pay the $2.60 with your return. Understanding how this tax works and learning with the advice of your accountant when is the best time to purchase products and services may save you money on your taxes. This tax applies to everything in your business so it is important to understand its implications.

Fuel tax is one of those mysterious taxes that Owner Operators may or may not know about depending on the company they're leased on with. You may have been working with the system and not even realized it. The fuel tax known as IFTA (International Fuel Tax Agreement) covers all of North America and is meant to even out road taxes paid by trucks to the Provinces and States they have traveled through. This changes constantly based on the areas traveled and is very hard to understand for most. Some companies do this for the Owner Operator, they may charge it back, or may count it against the fleet. Any Independent Operators will have to get this done on their own. It is a matter of recording the miles or kilometres traveled on each trip and charged against any fuel bought in that State or Province. For instance if you buy fuel in one State but don't travel very many miles through that State the money you paid may be counted against the miles you traveled in Ontario or another state. You can save money here if you look into the areas you run the most and calculate the best place to buy your fuel, however that calculation may not offset the price at the pumps. If you feel you are paying more fuel tax then doing some tracking in the way you operate, it may be the best use of your time.

Of course one of the problems of the road is that conditions are changing constantly whether it be weather related, traffic related, or economics. How you handle those situations is the reason some business survive and others fail. Winter is coming, hey this is Canada and there is no getting away from it unless you go on vacation. Winter is part of life here and can be very costly to those unaware of the conditions expected on the roadways. This is where the non professional Owner Operator gets into trouble. Did you see the news from Buffalo, they had quite a few snow storms that trapped drivers on the highway, the same thing happened on the 402 by Sarnia, the highway got shut down due to bad weather. As a professional driver this comes as part of the territory, but there are things you can do and should do to protect your business and bottom line as an Owner Operator. I realize that you can't predict mother nature and sometimes she can turn the world upside down on a dime, but I see it often where drivers do no trip planning, drive aimlessly on their trip and wonder why they get stuck, make no money, or get into wrecks due to bad weather. I am not talking about a little rain, or a few snow flakes, I am talking about Mother Nature's best work. What can you as an Owner Operator do to keep yourself out of harms way? The secret, planning!

Always keep your options open on how you will make your delivery safely. Idling in the middle of a closed highway will do nothing for the bottom line of your business. You are better off to be in a safe location such as a truck stop or motel than on the highway in a snow storm that has closed the road, as you watch your fuel gauge to make sure you have enough. How much fuel are you burning, trying to keep warm, What are the risks of someone causing an accident due to poor road conditions, or getting stuck in the spot your are sitting in? We all laugh at the four wheelers that don't plan when they get on the road, but how many of us drivers do the same things.

On my last road trip with my wife we were on a winter vacation and were returning home from the South. Watching the weather we knew we were going to cross possibly horrendous weather at some point as we approached the Great Lakes. Evaluating our options I decided to take a longer route home, but one that kept our options open almost all the way to the border. We ended up coming up through West Virginia. We monitored the weather throughout and made our decision to come out through Windsor Ontario. Knowing the road helped here as Interstate 90 was closed due to a major storm. We had bare roads all the way until we hit London Ontario but at this time we were close enough to get home. Had we stuck with our original plan we would have headed straight into the storm and been sitting on the interstate in Erie Pennsylvania. It is your duty as a professional driver to do proper trip planning and operate as safely as possible. It is your duty as an Owner Operator to protect your bottom line by running efficiently, saving resources, and making decisions on how to best keep your business out of trouble. Drive Safe!

Since we're talking resources after major expenses such as fuel and payroll tires come in high on the list. Tire expenses can eat half your budget if you don't pay attention to the basics. What is the trouble with tires? Their cost is one of the biggest concerns for the Owner Operator and trucking companies to get a handle on, but one of the most important pieces of operating profitably. The truth is that most Owner Operators don't put aside money for tires because they are not a daily operating expense. This especially true for the new Owner Operator that may have just bought a used truck and are struggling just to get miles down the road to create some income. If the driver hasn't set his business up properly to account for tire replacement then they will find themselves in a pickle down the road. This becomes even more important in the beginning stages when you first take over a truck and should be part of an overall checklist as to items that will need attention in the upcoming months.

Tires are like anything else, an investment and you get what you pay for. Buy old tires and you will have a low return on investment, by newer tires and the return on investment grows if managed correctly. However with so many manufacturers on the market how do you know which is the best tire for you giving you the best return on investment? The best place to start is with your trusted mechanic, take him or her a coffee and go ask them some questions about tire wear, casing and used tire buy back and so on. Be aware of what you should be looking for with your tires to spot potential problems. Find out how tires are traded and at what tread depth is the best time to trade to reap the most amount of money for your tire program. Once you have some first hand knowledge on what to look for and what is important the next step is to make sure you have the money set aside for a tire program. This is where most Owner Operators miss the bucket. This should be a part of your overall maintenance fund and costed out at each mile. The important part is to start this program even when you don't need tires because eventually you will. By having this money set side you can now be in a position to buy tires as the deals arise or from your preferred supplier giving you optimum pricing advantage over the person who buys them in the heat of a repair or incident. Don't forget to check out the supplier associated with your carrier as many times by buying within their plan you can get great savings for your equipment. If you operate in areas such as construction sites where the potential for tire problems are more common then a more aggressive tire program may be the answer to make sure you are operating in a safe manner.

If you watch your tires you will see that they are fairly predictable if you pay attention to them. Whenever I had dedicated equipment I was able to go years without tire problems, where many of my counterparts had tire recaps coming off on a regular basis. The most important factors for an effective tire program is to know how to gauge tire wear, the costs associated with returning casings and used tires, and to be putting money aside for repair and replacement as required. That being said for those that don't have too many trouble with tires, start asking questions about how to best use their maintenance money. Should I use my maintenance money for something else if I don't need it?

The answer in its most direct form-NO! It can be very tempting to start borrowing money from different areas when things get tight. My suggestion if at all possible is to leave that money alone because the day may come that you need that as well. So do you just let the account grow and hope for the best, of course not but if you have a proper budget in place then everything should be accounted for. Although maintenance is a variable expense for the sake of your budget it should be a fixed expense. What do I mean by that? Well you do your budget you should be putting a certain amount away for maintenance. The norm is around 10 cents per mile but that can also change based on the age of your truck, your truck payments, warranties, and so on. Since the average is 10 cents lets use that number. If you run 10,000 mile a month on average then your expense will be around $1000 per month for maintenance. Out of that will be your normal oil changes, grease jobs, headlights and other small items. So if you are doing things correctly you will probably spend about $500 on regular maintenance and the rest will sit in your account as equity. That remaining $500 should build and keep going until the day you need to replace tires, motor, etc. Hopefully nothing too drastic happens to your truck and you stay ahead of the game. So when should you use the money for something else? First of all make sure you go through this with your accountant because it will differ for every individual based on your tax situation, operating budget and so forth. But to give you a general outline here are my thoughts on the subject.

If you are just starting out, are still in your first truck, or have less than five years of experience in the industry then you should continue to let that money grow and not touch it. If you're on your second truck or further, have been an owner operator for a number of years then talk to your accountant and see whether you should move SOME of the money to pay for capital expenses, etc. This will be different for everyone so discussing your options with professional members of your team will help you to make a sound decision. I caution you though that even a newer truck can break down and it is important to make sure you have enough money to cover slow periods, breakdowns, towing, etc. Borrowing from the company should be your last resort. This is the part of being a business owner that is important to the cash flow and growth of your business and should not be decided on lightly.

Step 9

Compliance and Safety as an Owner Operator

CSA

stands for Comprehensive Safety Analysis. When CSA came into the fold in late 2010 its focus was on taking unsafe drivers off the road and targeting companies that were operating improperly and causing safety hazards. Companies enjoyed the switch on focus because it put more emphasis on the drivers to clean up their act. There was much talk about the rating aspect of the program and how it will affect drivers and job placement in the future, but what about the Owner Operator? What affect is CSA having on the bottom line of a company that has one or two trucks?

With CSA and a driver hired on by a fleet the safety focus is the primary concern. For the driver it is vital that by following the rules of the road and conditions outlined by CSA drivers will have career longevity and be safe operators. When an incident does happen because the driver is an employee many times the company will absorb the cost with a reprimand note put in the employees file. If an Owner Operator has an incident however the stakes change quite dramatically. Not only is the incident recorded and added to their file, but any money required for fines and clean up will most likely be charged back to the Owner Operator. Lets assume you received a fine for an infraction on the road. As an employee you may have to pay the fine or the company may pay the fine and the issue is finished. As an Owner Operator you will have to pay the fine, but since you are an independent contractor that money is either part of your operation budget or part of your profits. So even a fine of $500 changes your operating budget for the rest of the month by 5 cents per mile. It affects you for the rest of the month. Now you may not think that will have a major effect on your income but depending on the profit margin set out in your budget you may have wiped out your profits for the rest of the month. Many trucking companies operate on single digit profit margins of around six to nine percent. That may not sound like much but if the company is generating millions of dollars a year that is big money. If you're not paying attention to fines, infractions and other issues of CSA and your business you run the risk of eating your profits down to nothing.

Lets assume your profit from your business is $1000 per month above your expenses, you will have $12,000 at the end of the year in profit. If fines and other incidents eat up that money you have taken away all your profits, if you weren't planning on a profit margin then you have unexpectedly eaten up your operating budget. The success of your business depends on your bottom line. Money spent on fine would be better off spent on your maintenance budget. If you are receiving fines or having incidents on a regular basis you need to take a good hard look at your business. You may not be doing enough preventive maintenance, or your operating procedures may be out of line with your business. Either way the success of your business falls back into your hands.

Owner Operators have to watch compliance issues much more than employed drivers as you fall into the category of driver and possibly carrier depending on how your operation is set up. Learning how compliance can affect you and your operation is something every Owner operator should be on top of. If your company is not training you on safety and compliance on a regular basis then it is your duty to enroll or update yourself on a regular basis in order to meet compliance regulations. One of the basics that catch many people are the Controlled Basic that covers everything from drugs and alcohol to over the counter medications. Incorrect use of many medications can put drivers into a gray category to where they are in a compliance situation.

He was on his third round of the week and feeling very weak and sick. Josh had been fighting the cold he caught all week and things were getting worse, however he needed the miles so he kept chugging down the road. His truck looked like a medicine cabinet with tissues everywhere, over the counter cold medicine and orange juice bottles. He just wanted to go to bed for a few days. Josh kept humming along having a hard time staying awake with all the medicine. He continued down the road until arriving at the scale in Kentucky. He was asked to pull around for a routine check of his paperwork when the officer realized how out of it Josh seemed. Although Josh told them he had only taken cold medicine the officer asked for a drug test to be performed. While awaiting the drug test Josh sat next another driver that had been sought out for the same reason. This driver however was a little more nervous about the test as he had been drinking earlier before starting his shift and feared he may still have some in his system. As the drivers left the testing area, both were handed violations under the Controlled Substances Basic and ordered out of service for 8 hours. Josh's test came back positive due to the mixture of medicine he had taken which was causing the drowsiness. The other driver had failed to be alcohol free at least 4 hours before his shift. As the calls went out to their companies Josh's company told him they would fight it and to take the eight hours and get some rest. The other driver wasn't so lucky, he is now unemployed.

So many times we all have run into this situation where we are trying medications over the counter to help us feel better, however those medications that are there to make us feel better may be harming us more. They may seem to be harmless on their own but mixed with other medication can become a deadly drug, many make us drowsy and are made to help us sleep. If you aren't feeling well then the only way to make yourself better is through rest and sleep. Not easily done when on the road, but in the long run you are better to rest and lose a trip that week than to push it and possibly end up with problems like Josh. The Controlled Substance Basic is meant to curve drug use both illegal and legally. Make sure you know what you're taking and be cautious not to mix it with other drugs or alcohol. Your career and your health depend on it.

Sacrificing Security for Speed

Jim has been running most of the night and is getting tired. He has a couple more hours to go before reaching his destination and the thought of shutting down is really appealing to him at this point. He pulls into the restaurant parking area to grab a quick coffee to get him through the rest of the trip. He pulls into the front of the restaurant, puts on the air brakes and jumps out in a hurry to go get his coffee. While in the restaurant he gets into a short conversation with the waitress over her upcoming wedding and pays for his coffee, when he returns, his truck is gone! Dumbfounded he looks around in haste, darting back and forth from front of the building to the rear of the building, did he park it in an area that he forgotten? Is he losing his mind? Fearful that his truck has just been stolen he calls the police and informs them to what has happened. He then calls his company dispatch and General Manager to inform them to what has happened. As the investigation continues the truck was found later that day and had indeed been stolen in that split second that it was parked and Jim ran in for his coffee. The problem Jim came across from the insurance company was that he had left the truck running, and the keys in the ignition. By doing so they told him that he had not secured the truck properly leaving it open to theft.

In my 25 years of trucking I can't count how many times I have seen people leave their trucks running and go inside leaving it unattended. In older days the excuse was that it cost more to start the truck again than to leave it running. These days however, with electronics, and engine modifications it isn't cost effective or necessary to leave a truck running unattended. Now I know I am going to hear from the one person that says it should be left running because his alternator is acting up and the truck won't start again if shut off. I have been in that situation myself and you should get your alternator fixed. Now there are some instances when you may need to keep your truck running such as delivery situations and so on. For those situations you are best to have a second key that you can lock the truck from the outside while leaving it running.

In short you are best to always make sure you have secured your vehicle properly and that you know what's going on around it at all times. Do a check or walk around when leaving the vehicle and when returning to the truck later on. Security is the drivers responsibility, be careful where you park, be aware of your surroundings, and make sure your vehicle is secured or locked.

Theft is on the rise in many industries but especially the transport industry. This is due to various reasons from the economy to organized crime but the end result is the same. Crime is up and it is important as an industry partner, and professional drive that you do your part. In past years we would tell people we were running with where we were going, what we were hauling without a thought of a bad person listening to our conversation, after all bad people were busy planning or doing bad things, not listening to truckers on C.B.s. That has changed however and you now have to be aware of who may be on the other end of the radio. This really hit home for me when 9/11 happened. I was driving for a chemical company at the time and shortly after that incident we had some communications come out letting us know that our company and industry as a whole may be used as targets for supplies, etc. We were under strict orders not to communicate our company name, location, route, cargo, or anything else that may give away the vehicles we were driving. Knowing the chemicals that we were carrying and what they can do made me realize the situation we were in and how much security played a part in the larger scheme of things. If you have followed the reports in the media about the truck that got stolen while the police chased it around Ontario you may notice that it isn't even about the freight anymore. As I was watching that incident unfold I kept thinking to myself what would someone want with a load of wafer board? What kept crossing my mind is the fact that the truck may have been a decoy for another robbery taking place somewhere else. At the same time there were reports of a trailer being stolen somewhere else with a load of electronics. I don't know if they are connected, but it makes you wonder.

So how can you help prevent theft for your company? First don't tell people the type of cargo you have on as that may peak interest. Second, don't tell people the route you plan to take or your final destination so that an ambush cannot be planned. Third, lock your truck at all times even when driving too prevent roadside robberies. Fourth, secure your vehicle with locks, kingpins, and other mechanical measures to stave off robberies. Park in lighted and authorized areas or secure yards whenever possible. Fifth, be aware of your surroundings at all times. If anything looks suspicious report it and move on. Theft prevention is everyones problem from driver to taxpayer. Do your part to minimize the problem.

If there is one thing I hear people complain about is driving in pouring rain or bad weather. As commercial drivers we hit it all on a regular basis. Driving rain, icy roads, snow filled highways, and cold to hot temperature extremes. Add that to the fact that many of us run over large areas of North America and those weather changes can go from one form to another in the same run.

Recently on a road trip vacation with my wife we had switched letting her drive while I got some shut eye. Of course the weather changed on her and the rain got very bad. I, the sound sleeper that I am didn't hear a thing and probably drifted off into an even deeper sleep. Not wanting to wake me she kept forging ahead hoping it would come to a halt in short order. She focused on the advice I gave her on how I have handled bad weather for over 25 years in the seat of a truck. I have always told her to first relax. If you are uptight and scared you are going to get into an accident. I have a high temperament for bad weather and that helps. If you feel unsafe you are better to stop and get off the road than to push on, I have my 40 mile an hour rule that if I can't drive at least 40 miles an hour I am best parked in the truck stop waiting for better conditions. If I can drive through I turn on music that I enjoy, keep the C.B open for road communication and watch tires and steering wheel reactions to avoid hydroplaning. If the rain is a hard driving rain I tell people to keep going if they can see okay because a hard driving rain usually won't last long and you will run out of it. Many people down south pull off to the side however there are a couple of things wrong with that. It is more dangerous for you to be at the side of the road in bad weather, you may cause an accident by being on the road way. If you stop to wait it out you may be there a while if the system stays overhead for a while. So my wife following my advice made it through the driving rain successfully. She has always used that advice to get her through storms and it has worked for me often. Knowing your comfort level is the first step in making sure you are going to be operating safely in bad weather and techniques of course will depend on the road and weather.

I'll never forget that winter, it was one of the coldest on record. A deep freeze had fallen across all of North America and things were grinding to a halt. It didn't seem to matter where you bought your fuel, what type of truck you had, or how well maintained the truck was, Mother Nature was wreaking havoc. To add even more trouble to an already bad situation was the fact that Christmas was just days away and everyone was trying to get home for Christmas. I watched trucks pulling into the fuel bars at truck stops just puffing smoke, trying to get in and dump fuel additives in the tank trying to thaw out the freezing diesel fuel. Nothing seemed to protect you for long once you were down south of the Michigan line that year. Around every table was the conversation as to what is the best thing to put in your tanks to help, what shouldn't be done, what was the best kept secret. The answers could be haggled all night with no winner. I myself froze up in Indiana just south of Indianapolis, two miles from the truck stop. It took two days to get the truck into the shop, thats how long the line was to be thawed out. It took another day for the truck to thaw out and be ready to go. We were sleeping on pool tables and in the restaurant waiting for the trucks to be thawed out one by one. As a driver you may not have much option on the equipment you are given, but as an Owner Operator there may be things you can do.

I am amazed how much of the time drivers bounce up and down the road without the thought of breaking down, getting stuck in bad weather, or being delayed at a customer with nothing to eat. It happens everyday in trucking but many don't see it until it happens to them. Most seasoned veterans know what to expect and prepare ahead of time for the dangers of the road. Winter driving can teach all motorists a lot about being prepared for a trip, making sure our truck is maintained to prevent breakdowns, we are aware of the road ahead and where it leads us. Winter trains you to be professional from the other motorists on the road.

Those principles that make you prepare for life on the road in the winter can help your prepare for other areas of your business and life all year long. Think of business for example. With winter driving you didn't want to break down so you did preventive maintenance on your vehicle to get it ready for winter driving. By setting up your business with the proper management team, bookkeeper, and accountant you are setting it up with good advice to avoid breakdowns. By stocking your truck for winter driving with things like candles, blankets, food, clothing and other essentials you were prepared if you got stuck on the road and to shutdown due to weather issues. The same thing happens in business if you watch the cash flow in your business you are stocking up in case you have a bad month or have an emergency happen. By reading the map and understanding where you are going you are prepared for what lies ahead on the road to your destination. Business is the same way if you have a business plan you have a road map showing where you are going with your business and how you plan on getting there.

Winter teaches us a lot and the more we keep our eyes open and prepare properly the smoother the trip will be, winter teaches us many things, what has it taught you?

But common sense comes in many forms and sometimes it doesn't take bad weather or business profits to make things different, sometimes it just takes knowing how you may look to other people. Why not review the information on first impressions.

He is fifteen years old, almost six feet tall, and one hundred and ninety pounds. He looks double that size under a street lamp on a cold evening. He walks briskly in the cold trying to get home before curfew. Approaching from the opposite direction is a small woman, standing all of 5 foot, two inches tall. She is too is walking at a fast pace trying to get out of the cold night air, however she is even more in tune with her surroundings. The two walk head on in the dead of night on a lonely street, the blocks in the distance move closer together as the two people walk towards each other, until they are all but a block away from each other. The fifteen year old boy suddenly turns and crosses the street, why, was this the start of an attack? The woman notices the move and is relieved, she was wondering what would come of them once they passed in the night.

The fifteen year old boy in this story was me. I have come across that scenario most of my life and being this size in high school I realize that in the dark shadows of the night I probably look twice the size to a person that is smaller than me that can't see any details. People didn't realize that I was a nice guy, or that I would have helped them on a dime, that I was late and just in a hurry to get home, in the dark no one understands all that. I recognized it and was open to crossing the street if I saw a women coming up the same side of the street to relieve her stress because I understand she didn't know me.

The reason I tell you this story is that as professional drivers and owner operators we go through the same thing everyday. We intimidate many of the motorists on the road.

Now I don't believe we all do this and I don't believe we intend to do that when it does happen. It is just how we are perceived on the road, remember when something is smaller than you it will make you look twice the size. As cars get smaller for fuel economy, and our trucks get bigger and longer for freight capacity you can see how the intimidation factor increases. Add the problems of congested roadways, tight time lines, and everyday busyness of peoples lives and you have a recipe for disaster. Have you ever had a truck tailgating you when you are in the car, what do you see in the rear view mirror? You see a giant grill, you see a truck following too close, you see a possible accident situation. It happens everyday and is frightening to those who find themselves in that predicament. So what can you do to help avoid this situation?

The first thing is to recognize when you may seem intimidating to others. Many times you are in total control, have the right of way, but you will still come off as the aggressor just because of your size. In this day of cell phones and videos your actions may seem intimidating to someone not even involved in the situation. A professional driver operating safely will learn to back off and give people some space. Aim to change the views of the general public one car at a time by recognizing the intimidation factor.

What Will Your Profile Show?

There is a show that I enjoy, one of the few reality shows where millionaires are sent into poverty ridden environments for a week and have to find charities that they can help. Usually by the end of the show they have given away over $100,000 dollars and have had their eyes opened as to the struggling needs of others. If you have ever helped others you can see why this show is such an emotional experience.

Recently I was reading an article in the paper about a truck driver that had passed away in a crash after a 40 year driving career. The reporter went on to give a profile of his personal achievements, his warmheartedness to others, and his dedication to the industry. As I continued to read the article, I began to think about my career, the show I had watched on television and the accomplishments I have made through my life. Switching the name in the article I wondered what my profile might read when that day comes.

Now I am not asking you to focus on your passing in this life, nor do I think you will get into Heaven by doubling up on good deeds for the next few years, but it does get you thinking, what kind of profile will we read on you? What will people say about you when that final day comes along?

There are two ways you can think about it, you can focus on the end or you can focus on today. I prefer to focus on today. What allows you to sleep at night? Is it helping someone each day, is it knowing you did your best at your job, is it being there for your family? It may be different for each of us and that's okay, the point is you are comfortable as the human being you are. Most people will say that they don't care what people think of them and that's their choice, but in the end I think we all want to leave with a good name.

The reason I like the television show is it opens the eyes of the participants to the real world, and it also features the people who are stepping up everyday in their own way trying to make a difference. What most people don't realize is that you don't have to go that far off track to make a difference. All you have to do is have a positive influence on one person's life and it can be as simple as a "good morning." So what are some of the ways you can have a positive affect on others throughout your day?

First try being nice, just say hello and try to be a positive moment in someone's day. Compliment someone or help a person out. Be courteous on the road and help the industry in their fight to a brighter self image. Join a charity or a cause and help save a life. If you're a happy person just be yourself. Happy people attract others and make everyone's day a better place. Finally enjoy what you do and do it well. There is nothing worse to pull down your spirits than working in a job you don't like and doing it without any enthusiasm. So think about it, if we were reading about you for the last time, what would your profile say?

Step 10
Expanding Your Business for the Future

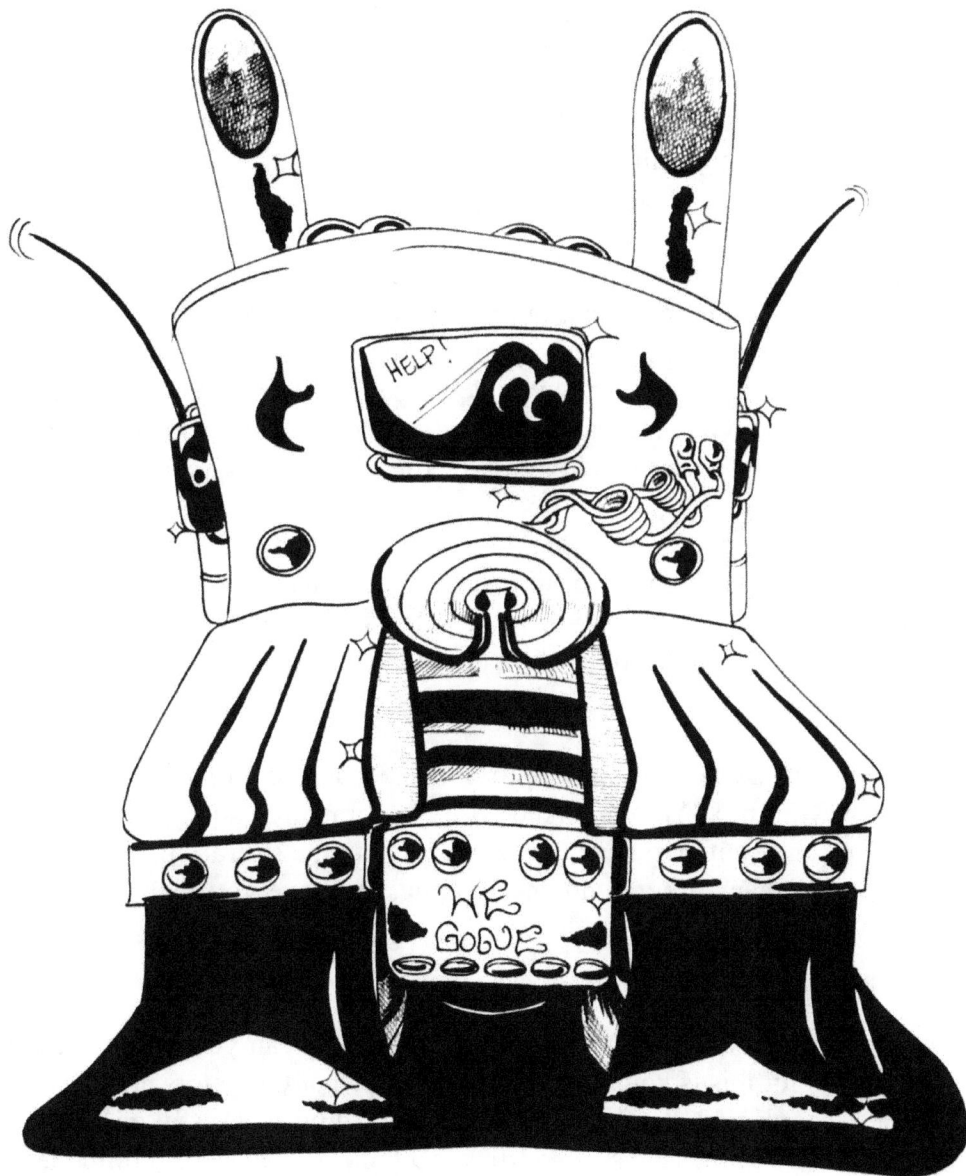

As I meet many owner operators in my travels many of them have lofty ideas of starting their own small fleet of two or three trucks. There is nothing wrong with that dream and since I am a big goal person I would rather work with someone who has goals than to work with those that have nothing planned out for the future. Having specific goals are great and that is the way everyone should work. It allows you to focus your business on items that will help you attain your goals. There is one problem for those of us that are extremely focused, sometimes we can grow too fast and cause more problems than needed. Adding trucks onto your business will drastically change the dynamics of how you operate, the amount of investment required, and develop roles in the company that you may be handling all by yourself.

Think about it, right now you are the owner, the office manager, the dispatcher, the driver, the janitor, the mechanic, and any other job you can possibly find for yourself. Once you start adding other people into the mix the dynamics change and that can make you take on positions you weren't planning on. For instance think about expanding your fleet to just one truck. You now have to hire another driver which will now add payroll duties, possibly dispatch (if you are totally independent) vacation fill in and so on. You may still be driving and able to handle that but your administration work will double with two trucks possibly causing you to outsource it.

Let's assume you move to two extra trucks, you may find you are starting to work outside of the truck. That's fine if you are planning on that but if you wanted to continue to drive it may be an area you are uncomfortable with. At this point you may also need more administration staff and depending how your business is set up you may find yourself now doing sales to find enough work for the trucks. You may also have to start adding more overhead to your business, parking issues, maintenance issues, and office space can add more overhead than most people plan on.

Now going back to the beginning I don't want to scare you. Many of these issue may go away depending on how you are operating your business. If you're leased on with a carrier then maybe parking, maintenance, dispatch, and sales may not be an issue. Bookkeeping and other office administrative tasks can be outsourced. The trick is to have a plan in place of how you will handle expansion.

You have been a successful Owner Operator with one truck and feel that it is time to expand by adding another truck to your mix. You've talked with the company and because you have been a star driver for them they are excited to have you add a truck to the operation. You don't feel it will be hard to find a driver as many are around and looking, but have you really thought the hiring process out as far as you should?

Just because you have been successful with one truck doesn't mean you will be successful with another truck. The reason for this is you! I talk with many Owner Operators and they feel because they are good business people with the first truck that they will be successful with the their second truck. The reality is that many times the second truck is a failure because the component that made the first truck a success is removed from the picture.

That component is you! You are not there every minute of the day making those smart decisions that kept your operation successful. The second driver may drive a certain way that doesn't give you as good a fuel economy as you would like, or isn't as clean as you would like them to be. No one takes the same care with your equipment as you do because they have no vested interest in the success of the business other than their job. What I hear from many business owners looking to expand is the fact that they feel they can help make those decisions over the phone but in reality if you are driving a truck yourself you may not have the time, or be able to monitor that second driver every minute. It takes good time management to operate one truck successfully, two trucks takes extreme time management. Where many go wrong is right at the beginning with the hiring stage. Many hire friends or relatives and that can usually turn out badly. So how do you start the process of expanding?

Planning is the first key, I find Owner Operators will spend time looking around at trucks getting the best deal for their money and then hire anyone that comes along to operate it. Take your time and start building up your network of potential drivers ahead of time so you have a pool of quality candidates. Realize when you are ready to hire you will have to take time out from running your own truck to hire and train the driver for the second one. Partner with schools to create a list of future candidates. When planning for the second truck many price the wage for the second truck very low to try to increase profits, you will need to meet the market wage at least to get quality drivers. The only way to adjust this is if you have some type of escrow arrangement for buying into the truck later if that is an option. Make sure you have money built into your budget for all expenses and never miss a payment on someones wages. That will be the kiss of death. Owning multiple trucks is a daunting task at best and the successful ones have planned for problems and the start up phase. Your income on that truck will increase overtime providing quality drivers fill the seat. The best place to start is with your own profit and loss statement and some planning time.

Qualifying Your Road Buddy

There is nothing worse than working with people you dislike. We all do it and it can be a real drag. With a recruiting shortage many carriers are looking for multiple drivers and your carrier is probably the same. What many drivers don't realize is that you can help your carrier get top quality people before they even apply to the recruiting department.

How many times have we as drivers been running down the road talking with fellow drivers we meet in our travels. I know over the 25 year driving career that I had I have talked with hundreds of drivers. Many of those have asked what the company I was driving for was like to work at. As we rolled down the road relaying the great points about being employed by the company we usually don't give much thought as to who the person is that we are telling all of this to. As drivers many of us assume that the recruiting department will check all their credentials and if they pass the test then it is out of our hands. What you don't realize is that you have much more control than that. You can be qualifying these guys before they even apply.

How would you feel if you are talking with his driver and answering his questions and he starts to get on your nerves, after a while you have had enough of him and then voila, he is employed a month later working at your company? I know, I would feel the same way. Now I don't expect you to qualify everyone and don't expect your company to hire only the person that you select or your would be the head of recruiting. The point is that many times you can tell if a new candidate will be a good fit for your company. If you have a good standing with your company then they will respect your opinion and take that into account. I have worked at many companies, more of the small ones that had no problem asking other drivers if the new candidate would fit with the company culture. If no one liked him things wouldn't be getting any better. If the guy asking about your company is driving ahead of you and his truck isn't maintained or he is driving all over the road then those are some clear signs that he may not fit on the team of a company with highly polished equipment.

If you find that many drivers are asking about your company then you may want to talk with recruiting and find a question you could ask about a situation a driver may find themselves in and ask that particular question. If they answer correctly they may be a good fit, if not don't tell them any contact information. If you have been working at your company for a while don't be afraid to be very selective about who you recommend. You have to work there too! This is even more important if you are looking for a driver for your own fleet. Getting into employees is a very different area than being the only person you need to worry about. Once you decide to hire for another truck or to help in the office make sure you know who you are working with. Be an objective recruiter and distance yourself from any friendship if one exists. You may find your friendship, your business, and everything else at risk.

Summary

*T*here is no secret for success, no formula that if followed will make us all rich. The reason is that common sense, a business mentality, and experience in the industry is what makes a successful business. The entrepreneurial spirit is alive and well in North America and the people you believe in are the ones that will provide the most guidance in that endeavor. Whether you listen to me or another person that you respect remember in the end it comes down to one person, you! We can only guide you with information, share experiences with you, and hope that you learn from your own mistakes. There will be many as you go down the road of a professional truck driver and even more so as a business owner known as an Owner Operator. The successful ones will be the people that learn from those mistakes and move forward.

Some Owner Operators won't listen, they think they have the answers, but in many of my presentations I ask the question, who has a proper business plan and almost every person says they don't think they need one. Not only do you need one, but it is the first step in a successful operation. You don't need a fifty page document full of corporate speak, you need a road map. A simple guideline that has all the information you need to make sure you are running a successful business. Many people in this industry are working hard to bring new life to the industry. As the veterans grow older and retire, new blood is needed, new technology is available, and new processes are in the works. Those that embrace change will be the successful Owner Operators of tomorrow.

This book is set out for you to follow much like a road map. Start at step one and do your homework, then move onto step two and so on. The only way you wouldn't be successful in this industry is if you choose not to listen to the information that is laid out in this book. I suggest reading the book, then go out and get the information required. Ask questions of qualified people and don't listen to the loudmouths or the unsuccessful.

I wish you well in your journey and future success. The industry depend on it.

Bruce Outridge
Transportation Consultant

Bruce's first look into the world of transportation began at the age of seventeen and seemed to come into his own with the world of transportation. Starting in the moving industry anyone like Bruce was regarded as a prime candidate to carry furniture out of your house. He didn't come from a long line of truck drivers, in fact in his household nobody knew what a truck was. His Dad was a hard working accountant, his Mum worked for the airline. He just needed a job; there was no grand plan at that point.

From day one in the industry he learned the importance of customer service; the public is good for that – training! His father brought him up with a great work ethic and that carried him through life to this day. He moved up and become a driver for the company eventually moving from Atlas Van Lines to North American Van Lines. As a driver he was paid a percentage for regional moves and learned the art of negotiating with helpers for pay, assessing costs for trips, and time management. He moved further into his career, got his "A" license and owned his own truck with a partner at the ripe young age of 20 years old. He later decided to move to the freight side of the industry and started in the city working for local trucking companies, one now known as Manitoulin Transport. From there through a connection he started his highway career hauling magazines throughout the US for a private carrier. He loved that job and finally felt his dream of working with the big trucks and all the chrome had been attained. After the company shrunk its fleet Bruce moved over to a smaller company where he learned the art of driver, dispatcher, and more. Unhappy there he began with J. Syvret & Co continued to run North America for the next six years. He enjoyed those years but kids came along and he found he wanted to be home more. He had looked into returning to the ranks of Owner Operator, when an opportunity came up to run for a private carrier again and he joined the forces of Nalco Canada with their Chemtrak fleet. Having hauled chemicals for most of his career and his customer service skills moved him up the corporate ladder quickly finally arriving as Team Leader for the fleet. He flourished in that position but frustration with company policies caused him to leave after a 13 year employment with the company. He took the daring leap into entrepreneurship.

In 2003 he had started an art business part time and after leaving his job in 2006 he decided to proceed full time with Bruce Outridge Productions doing editorial illustration, cartoons, caricatures, and more. Realizing he enjoyed public speaking and 25 years of knowledge that he could share with new drivers and Owner Operators he opened Outridge Consulting Services in 2009. Bruce now spends time operating both divisions as needs arise. He absolutely loves being an entrepreneur, being creative, and helping people. After adding Outridge Translation Services they tied all the divisions' into their parent company Outridge Enterprises Inc. The businesses have since launched many products and services from cartoon strips for many of the industry magazines to publications to representing the OS Program for Owner Operators. Bruce writes columns and blogs for many industry magazines and businesses and offer presentations and training for clients in business and leadership. In 2011 he was honoured as a recipient of the "Trucking Ambassador of the Year Award" by the Road Today Media Group. People ask why he is still in the industry when he doesn't have to be. He says the answer is simple, the people. For more information on Bruce visit his website www.outridge.ca or www.bruceoutridge.com

Biography by Carmen Outridge

Running by the Mile - 10 Steps to a Successful Trucking Business